LETTERS FROM THE DARKLING PLAIN

UNIVERSITY OF MISSOURI STUDIES LVIII

LETTERS FROM THE
DARKLING PLAIN

LANGUAGE AND THE GROUNDS

OF KNOWLEDGE IN THE POETRY

OF ARNOLD AND HOPKINS

HOWARD W. FULWEILER

UNIVERSITY OF MISSOURI PRESS

Copyright materials from the works of Gerard Manley
Hopkins, *The Poems of Gerard Manley Hopkins*, 4th ed.,
W. H. Gardner and N. H. MacKenzie, eds.; *Letters of
Gerard Manley Hopkins to Robert Bridges*, rev. ed.,
Claude Colleer Abbott, ed.; *The Sermons and Devotional
Writings of Gerard Manley Hopkins*, Christopher
Devlin, S.J., ed.; *The Journals and Papers of Gerard Manley
Hopkins*, Humphry House, ed.; and *The Correspondence
of Gerard Manley Hopkins and Richard Watson Dixon*,
Claude Colleer Abbott, ed., have been used by
permission of the publisher, the Oxford University
Press by arrangement with the Society of Jesus.

FOR MY MOTHER

ACKNOWLEDGMENTS

I have been working on this book longer than its brevity might indicate, and my obligations are considerable. I should especially like to thank Mr. Owen Barfield for reading an early version of the manuscript and making incisive comments on it.

I am also indebted to many friends and colleagues at the University of Missouri who read or listened to various drafts of the manuscript and gave me valuable advice—especially to Professor Arthur Schwartz, now of the University of California at Santa Barbara; Professor Roger Meiners, now of Michigan State University; Professor Richard Hocks; and Professor James Heldman.

I am grateful to Professors Jerome Beaty of Emory University and Donald Smalley of the University of Illinois for their careful reading of the manuscript and for their intelligent suggestions for improving it.

My thanks are due to the Research Council of the University of Missouri for providing me with summer research leaves during which I was able to do preliminary study for the book.

Finally, I should like to express my gratitude to Mrs. Rose McClure, the English Department Secretary, who for several years was the unfailing support of a chairman attempting to write.

H. W. F.
Columbia, Missouri
June, 1972

CONTENTS

I.

POETRY AND THE
PROBLEM OF LANGUAGE

In his perceptive book on Dante, *The Figure of Beatrice*, Charles Williams describes Dante's sensibility in a striking and suggestive way. Of Beatrice, the crowning symbol of the *Divine Comedy,* he writes: "She is, in the whole *Paradiso*, his way of knowing, and the maxim is always 'look; look well.' Attention is demanded of him and her expositions are the result of his attention. She is, in a sense, his very act of knowing. It is in this sense that the *Paradiso* is an image of the whole act of knowing which is the great Romantic Way, the Way of the Affirmation of Images, ending in the balanced whole. Indeed the entire work of Dante, so interrelevant as it is, is a description of the great act of knowledge, in which Dante himself is the Knower, and God is the Known, and Beatrice is the Knowing."[1]

Dante's poetic vision, as Williams describes it, derives from an older, more nearly unified consciousness. For Dante, the symbols of his poem are the *way* he knows, are in fact the knowing itself. He did not conceive of his poem as an ornamental exercise somehow allegorizing a separate, autonomous, and objective "truth." Nor did he think of the *Divine Comedy* as simply an expression of his own soul in the manner of, say, Poe. Instead, he seems to have regarded the poem as a creative mode of perceiving reality.

Another influential student of the medieval consciousness, Erich Auerbach, has arrived at somewhat similar conclusions, supported by a solid foundation of scholarship and applicable to a broad range of earlier

1. *The Figure of Beatrice: A Study in Dante* (New York, Farrar, Straus & Giroux, Inc., 1961), 231.

11

literature. I refer to Auerbach's important work on the figural interpretation of Scripture and its later application to poetry—especially that of Dante. In the Middle Ages the figural approach to the literature of the Bible involved interpreting the significance (for the interpreter) of two actual historical events or persons in relation to each other. Thus Moses and Christ are related as "figure and fulfillment. The fulfillment is often designated as *veritas* . . . and the figure correspondingly as *umbra* or *imago*, but both shadow and truth are abstract only in reference to the meaning first concealed, then revealed; they are concrete in reference to the things or persons which appear as vehicles of the meaning. Moses is no less historical and real because he is an *umbra* or *figura* of Christ, and Christ, the fulfillment, is no abstract idea, but also a historical reality."[2]

It is true that medieval literature provided a variety of figural, allegorical, and symbolic forms, all of which, applied to classical as well as Christian material, occur in the *Divine Comedy*.[3] All three forms were more closely related in the Middle Ages than they are today. Although, for one matter, allegorical significance in a work is now thought to be quite different from symbolic or figural significance, there is no doubt, as Auerbach argues, that "for certain groups in medieval spirituality, allegory meant something more real than it does for us; in allegory people saw a concrete realization of thought, an enrichment of possibilities of expression." In Dante's treatment of Saint Francis's marriage with Lady Poverty in the *Paradiso*, for instance, "Dante . . . introduces one single allegorical figure, Poverty, and connects her with a historical, that is to say, a concrete real personality. . . . He draws the allegory into actual life, he connects it closely with historical fact."[4]

2. "Figura," in *Scenes from the Drama of European Literature* (Gloucester, Mass., Peter Smith, 1959), 34.
3. "Figura," in *Scenes*, 64.
4. "St. Francis of Assisi in Dante's 'Commedia,' " in *Scenes*, 82–83.

The sense of actuality, of concrete reality, brought about by Dante's use of *figurae* is even stronger elsewhere in the poem. Cato of Utica, for example, whose choice of suicide ironically prefigures Christian freedom, is "not an allegory like the characters from the *Roman de la Rose*, but a figure that has become the truth." Similarly, Virgil was for Dante a *figura* of the "poet–prophet–guide, now fulfilled in the other world."[5]

For Dante, thus, the literal meaning of an event or the historicity of a figure did not conflict with its deeper spiritual meaning, but enhanced and validated it. I am reminded of Owen Barfield's argument in his brilliant *Speaker's Meaning:* that the semantic splitting of words into "literal" and "figurative" meanings is of very recent origin. When we use the word *heart* to signify both a physical organ and the inner feelings of a man, we must not assume that we are inventing a metaphor in the second instance, but only that we are using the word historically. Although *heart* has always had both a physical and a spiritual or nontangible meaning, both meanings were until recent times considered of equal reality and mutually supportive.[6]

A careful reading of Dante, especially in the light of critics of such diverse views as Auerbach and Williams, must leave us with the conclusion that he aimed, as T. S. Eliot has said, "to set something down. . . . [He] succeeded in dealing with his philosophy, not as a theory (in the modern and not the Greek sense of that word) or as his own comment or reflection but in terms of something perceived."[7] Dante did not think of himself as writing a poem only for its autonomous aesthetic value, or as fulfilling a need for self-expression, or as making palatable a truth separate from the symbols of the poem.

5. "Figura," in *Scenes*, 65–67, 69.
6. *Speaker's Meaning* (Middletown, Conn., Wesleyan University Press, 1967), 56–59.
7. *The Sacred Wood: Essays on Poetry and Criticism* (London, Methuen & Co., Ltd., 1960), 170, 171.

His conception of his role was in some respects more like that of Darwin as he wrote *The Origin of Species*: "setting down something perceived."

It is apparent that Dante's assumptions about poetry and the creative process are not commonplace in the nineteenth and twentieth centuries; it is equally apparent that the assumptions Dante rejected or of which he was unaware have become literary commonplaces in the past two hundred years. Present-day readers perceive in them "art for art's sake" and its many manifestations, from French symbolism to certain new criticism. Here, also, are the self-expressive agonies of some kinds of "romantic" poetry, from Shelley falling on the thorns of life to the therapeutic outpourings of the radical Left or the Beat Generation. Finally, operating in contemporary readers' attitudes is the widespread belief that poetry is a rhetorical adornment used to help convey messages essentially unrelated to the poetry itself: Martin Tupper, James Whitcomb Riley, or Rod McKuen come to mind. The assumption that the poet's task is analogous to Darwin's is *not* characteristic. Several generations of literary apologists have devoted their lives to separating poetry from the class of knowledge-producing activities.

Although Williams, Eliot, and Auerbach were describing the poetic theory and practice of a medieval consciousness, their words bear considerable relevance for the study of nineteenth-century poetry. As Barfield has recognized the semantic splitting of words into "literal" and "spiritual" meanings, so we must recognize the development of a parallel division between two types of sensibility—one that defines the function of poetry as strictly limited to self-expression, pure aesthetics, or ornamentation, and one that discerns poetry as a mode of knowing reality, whether through the power of symbolic forms, or through the figural significance of history itself, or both. It is this dichotomy that has so clouded our understanding of the role of poetry for the past two centuries. This confusion is especially true of the nineteenth century, when the split first came to be recognized.

The shift in sensibility that took place between the Middle Ages and the nineteenth century has sometimes been ascribed to the intellectual revolution of the seventeenth century, a proposition with which I generally agree. If we are to accept Susanne Langer's conclusions, the central generative concept of that revolution is the theory of knowledge developed by John Locke (shared in many respects by Hobbes and Bacon).[8] Locke's basic premise is the conscious bifurcation of nature into an inner and outer realm: a division between observer and observed, perceiver and perceived, subject and object. A corollary of this thesis is the autonomy of the external world, which is separate from its perceiver and which implants itself upon the blank "white paper" of the human mind—to use Locke's celebrated metaphor. Since, in this theory, reality tends to be external to the perceiver, cognition depends upon the senses, which are conceived as passive receptors. Such a theory of knowledge has a profound impact on one's attitude toward language. If external "things" are reality, independent of human perception, words should be parallel signs for things, or at least signs for human ideas of the things from which the ideas derived. They must be permanent, abstract counters that "stand for" external reality itself or at least a static concept of reality. This theory caused Locke to reject what he called "allusive," "figurative," or "ornamental" language—what we are often likely to describe as "symbolic" or "mythic" language. Whereas for Dante the figurative meaning of an event or a word and its literal meaning were mutually validating and organically fused, for Locke the two meanings were necessarily divided, and one—the figurative—was to be rejected. Whereas the medieval poet saw both *figura* and *littera* as realities equally partaking of and producing *veritas*, the seventeenth-century philosopher saw *figura* as an empty distor-

8. *Philosophy in a New Key: A Study in the Symbolism of Reason, Rite, and Art* (New York, Mentor Books, 1958), 26.

tion of *littera,* which in proper speech should by itself produce *veritas.*

Analogies to Locke's view of language may be found in many places in the seventeenth century. The influential comments on style by Thomas Sprat, the historian of the Royal Society, are instructive: *"Eloquence* ought to be banish'd out of all *civil* Societies, as a thing fatal to Peace and good Manners. . . . [Ornaments of speaking] are in open defiance against *Reason;* professing, not to hold much correspondence with that; but with its Slaves, the Passions." The Royal Society resolved "to return back to the primitive purity, and shortness, when men deliver'd so many *things,* almost in an equal number of *words."* [9] The noncreative and static quality of his theory was made plain by Locke when he likened the inner world of simple ideas to the "world of visible things, where in [man's] power, however managed by art and skill, reaches no farther than to compound and divide the materials that are made to his hand but can do nothing towards making the least particle of new matter, or destroying one atom of what is already in being."[10] Outside the circle of imaginative literature and literary criticism, this theory of language still seems to be the accepted one. Words must be the stable counters for reflecting and communicating an already existent reality: either external reality itself or internal nonverbal ideas derived from external reality. Twentieth-century linguistic philosophers like Carnap, Wittgenstein—at least the early Wittgenstein—or Ayer tell us that language concerned with matters other than the external world has no significance.[11] The views of

9. *History of the Royal Society,* Jackson I. Cope and Harold Whitmore Jones, eds. (St. Louis, Washington University, 1958), 111–13.
10. *Essay Concerning Human Understanding,* Alexander Campbell Fraser, ed. (Oxford, The Clarendon Press, 1894), Vol. I, Book II, chap. ii, sec. 2.
11. Wittgenstein wrote, for instance, "Most propositions and questions, that have been written about philosophical matters, are not false, but senseless. We cannot, therefore, answer ques-

modern positivist philosophers seem to support Locke's own statement that "figurative speech" is an "abuse of language."[12]

The insistence on "so many words, so many things," without figurative "cheats" (to use Locke's term), is not restricted to science or positivist philosophy, but has also been common even in idealist philosophy. T. S. Eliot, for instance, wrote of the followers of Hegel that they "have as a rule taken for granted that words have definite mean-

---

tions of this kind at all, but only state their senselessness. Most questions and propositions of the philosophers result from the fact that we do not understand the logic of our language," in *Tractatus Logico–Philosophicus* (London, K. Paul, Trench, Trubner & Co., 1922), 63. Similarly, Rudolf Carnap dismissed the cognitive value of poetry: "Many linguistic utterances are analogous to laughing in that they have only an expressive function, no representative function. Examples of this are cries like 'Oh, Oh,' or, on a higher level, lyrical verses. The aim of a lyrical poem in which occur the words 'sunshine' and 'clouds,' is not to inform us of certain meteorological facts, but to express certain feelings of the poet and to excite similar feelings in us," in *Philosophy and Logical Syntax* (London, K. Paul, Trench, Trubner & Co., 1935), 28, 29. Alfred Ayer, like Locke, bases cognition on "sense–content": "It is only by the occurrence of some sense–content, and consequently by the truth of some observation–statement, that any statement about a material thing is actually verified." Knowledge depends on experience. "For I require of an empirical hypothesis, not indeed that it should be conclusively verifiable, but that some possible sense–experience should be relevant to the determination of its truth or falsehood," in *Language, Truth and Logic*, 2d ed. (London, Victor Gollancz, Ltd., 1956), 12 and 31.

12. A portion of Locke's long statement reads as follows: "Since wit and fancy find easier entertainment in the world than dry truth and real knowledge, figurative speeches and allusion in language will hardly be admitted as an imperfection or abuse of it. . . . But yet, if we would speak of things as they are, we must allow that all the art of rhetoric, besides order and clearness, all the artificial and figurative application of words eloquence hath invented, as for nothing else but to insinuate wrong ideas, move the passions, and thereby mislead the judgment; and so indeed are perfect cheats," in *Human Understanding*, Vol. II, Book III, chap. x, sec. 34.

17

ings, overlooking the tendency of words to become indefinite emotions. (No one who had not witnessed the event could imagine the conviction in the tone of Professor Eucken as he pounded the table and exclaimed *Was ist Geist? Geist ist. . . .*) If verbalism were confined to professional philosophers, no harm would be done. But their corruption has extended very far."[13]

In its relation to art, the Lockian revolution in epistemology and its corollary effect on language made the unified symbolic consciousness of Dante difficult or impossible for nineteenth- and twentieth-century poets to share. Whereas Dante regarded the verbal symbols of the *Divine Comedy* as creative means to knowing, later poets would have to live with a proposition foreign to Dante: that poetry is an ornamental rhetoric separate from "real" truth or is simply self-expressive. Whereas Dante could believe, in modern philosophical terminology, that poetry is cognitive, the moderns would have to deal with the popular assumption that only scientific statement conveys knowledge of reality.

There thus came to be a profoundly uneasy relation between "words," "things," the "self," and what we may call "reality," "truth," or even "fact," depending on the context. This uneasiness came about as a result of the sharper philosophical and psychological analysis that grew out of the intellectual revolution initiated in the seventeenth century. From a more disquieting perspective, however, the new sophisticated articulation and analysis could be seen as a philosophical and psychological fragmentation. An increasing concern with language and epistemology toward the end of the eighteenth century created a serious literary problem: What is the function of poetry? If the sensationalists were right, poetry could be no more than ornament superadded to prose statement, or (as one twentieth-century positivist explains) simply a higher level of expressive cries like "Oh, Oh!" What made dealing with the dilemma so traumatic was

13. *Sacred Wood*, 9.

that it had never really been faced before. True, Plato had scorned the poets as imitators of imitations, but there had never been the precisely articulate categorization that grew from the scientific revolution, or the confident assertion of scientists and utilitarians alike that what appeared to be "there" to the senses was truly there and was all that *was* there—in the older terminology, *littera* equals *veritas.* The problem was acute because of the solid intellectual advance upon which it was based. It is almost a truism to say that there could not have been the fragmentation of words, things, reality, and the self if Locke and others had not managed to make important distinctions between them in human consciousness.

*   *   *   *

A theory of knowledge so powerful as that of Locke evoked its antithesis in the subjective empiricism of Berkeley and especially in the idealism of Kant and the German transcendentalists of the late eighteenth and early nineteenth centuries. Instead of assuming that reality is "out there," they tended to assume that it is "in here," or that only phenomena were accessible to human perception while reality remained mysterious. A counterproposition, the inevitable complement to Locke's theory, thus emerged for those who were dissatisfied with the positivist Lockian thesis. Kant made clear that external reality is only appearance and is determined by the categories of knowing available to the knower. In fact, a common conclusion (not necessarily Kant's view) was that reality, for human use at any rate, is found only in the inner subjective realm—a view as foreign to Dante's as that of Locke. In general, then, the division of the world into outer and inner realms produced, by the end of the eighteenth century, two polar theories: one that declared reality to be external and one that defined it as internal.

It is not surprising, in this circumstance, that the study of the romantic movement in literature has concerned itself with the relation of poetry to these two theories of knowledge. Romantic poets, by and large, felt more at home with the internal than with the external—from Blake's violent rejection of Locke and all his works, to the trimming modifications of Hartleyan association-ism by Wordsworth, to Coleridge's elaborate explanation of the creative imagination. A characteristic romantic response to the split was to stop regarding poetry as an abstract reflection of a supposed external reality and to begin developing an "expressive" theory of art, to move, in short, from the mirror to the lamp—to borrow Meyer Abrams' suggestive phrase. A poet was not to be thought of as a recording tablet but as an autonomous fountain. This view of art, taken by itself, has developed into a pervasive modern attitude toward poetry. Although early eighteenth-century aesthetics held that poetry at least reflected reality, at least held the mirror up to life, roman-tic critics and artists sometimes acted as though it were only expressive. Nevertheless, in all of them—especially in Blake, Wordsworth, and Coleridge—there is an abid-ing preoccupation with the problem of poetry not only as self-expression but as a valid means to knowledge.

*   *   *   *

The literary dilemma precipitated by the epistemo-logical and linguistic revolution of the seventeenth and eighteenth centuries and the romantic response to it of the early nineteenth has been a common subject of liter-ary and philosophical discussion for the past thirty or forty years. The discussion has tended, however, to limit itself to the great romantics. It has been frequently as-sumed either that English romanticism "never grew up" to fulfill its early promise or that the Victorians failed to build on the romantic foundations. Early twentieth-cen-tury criticism sometimes charged the romantics with irre-sponsible infantilism under the first heading and the Vic-torians with insensitive Philistinism or sentimental distortion under the second. Although these charges have not been leveled with their original ferocity in the last few years, criticism of the Victorians has less regularly considered them in the light of the profound epistemological changes that so affected the great romantics. Yet there is an obvious need for investigation of this kind.

The literary historian could wish to know more about the origins of the modern sensibility in figures like Poe, Swinburne, Rossetti, the French symbolists, or even Alfred Austin or Martin Tupper. It would be illuminating to see these figures in their total philosophical context. Why did Poe so solemnly assert that truth and poetry are like oil and water? What is the larger significance of what Allen Tate has so acutely described as Poe's "angelic imagination" in opposition to the "symbolic imagination" of Dante?[14] If "Eureka" is, as it seems to be, an apologia for a curious mixture of self-expression and autonomous aestheticism as the justification for art, what does this fact suggest for the general role of poetry in the modern world? Further, why did Swinburne live, as Eliot described his situation, in a "world of words," where only "the word . . . gives him the thrill, not the object. When you take to pieces any verse of Swinburne, you find that the object was not there—only the word."[15]

The answer may be that the aesthetics of both Poe and Swinburne are directly related to the fragmentation of words, things, self, and reality occasioned by Locke's revolution and the subsequent splitting of poetic sensibility.

As interesting as a wider study of the relation of Victorian linguistic and aesthetic theory to epistemology might prove, I have focused mine on two of the major Victorian poets, Matthew Arnold and Gerard Manley Hopkins. Arnold must be regarded as one of the most representative of his period and Hopkins one of the most complex. The poetic careers of both men are structured

14. See *Collected Essays* (Denver, The Swallow Press, 1959), 413.
15. *Sacred Wood*, 147, 148.

in good part by their internal conflicts. One cannot think of Arnold without contrasting the urbane, disinterested critic with the alienated prophet of the darkling plain; Hopkins is not only the ecstatic praiser of God in nature but also the agonized and isolated author of "dead letters sent / To dearest him that lives alas! away."

The works of these two writers are especially appropriate for linguistic and epistemological study because we find in them an unusually large amount of theorizing about the function of poetry and language—implicit in their poetry and explicit in Arnold's formal criticism and in Hopkins' letters and journals. It is a striking fact that their theorizing is itself as internally divided as the obvious polarities within each man's career. The general thesis of this book is that the racking conflicts and painful doubts of Arnold and Hopkins about the role of poetry in the modern world—and in their own lives—were brought about in large part by the philosophical dilemma we have been discussing and, further, that their careers illuminate the problem with enormous and sometimes horrifying clarity.

The two related studies attempt to show how two major Victorian poets faced the dilemma of language in a changed world and devoted the greater share of their creative energies to establishing under new conditions the grounds of knowledge in relation to the function of poetic art. In their efforts can be seen the gravity of the epistemological and linguistic revolution and its pervasive influence on the other concerns of the modern world, as the definitive formation of that world began in the nineteenth century. There were in both poets explicit analogies to the implicit epistemological problem that so concerned them. It has been said that there are only two topics of abiding and universal interest: sex and theology. Perhaps it is emblematic of the centrality of Arnold and Hopkins that sex and theology should be their analogies. In Arnold—as in Dante—the continuing analogy is to romantic love and the possibility of valid human communication in a mechanical world. For Hopkins the

22

analogy is theology; like Dante, he attempted to use his poetry as a means of knowing and achieving a new relationship with God. Both poets were deeply aware of their "modernity" and conceived of themselves as creating a new kind of poetry—a poetry fit for a new age. Both created an imaginative poetry of knowledge although—thoroughly post-Lockian men that they were—Arnold came to fear that poetry was illusory and Hopkins to suspect it as a possible occasion of sin.

II.

MATTHEW ARNOLD: THE CITY OF GOD WITHOUT BEATRICE

Ah! two desires toss about
The poet's feverish blood.
One drives him to the world without,
And one to solitude.
> "Stanzas in Memory of the
> Author of 'Obermann.' "

Hither and thither spins
The wind-borne, mirroring soul,
A thousand glimpses wins,
And never sees a whole. . . .
> "Empedocles on Etna"

POETRY AS KNOWLEDGE VS. POETRY AS *Aberglaube*

If the method of modern poetry is mythic, as Eliot
has said, Matthew Arnold's poetry must be regarded as
a touchstone of modern literature as it so often is of
Victorian. If we are sometimes confused as to the meaning of his work, we are increasingly aware of its continuing life as a mythic representation that attempts to come

Portions of this chapter appeared as "Matthew Arnold: The
Metamorphosis of a Merman" in *Victorian Poetry*, I, No. 3
(August 1963), 208–22. Copyright © 1963 by West Virginia
University and reprinted here by permission of the publisher
and of the editor, John F. Stasný.

to grips with the hard realities of our "darkling plain" through the imaginative categories of the strayed reveller, the abandoned merman, the suicidal Greek philosopher, and the elusive scholar-gipsy who extends his life by not living it. Professor Dwight Culler, in his excellent critical treatment of Arnold's poetry, has attempted to reconcile these various poetic attitudes by ordering them into a unified imaginative structure, a consistent and pervasive Arnoldian myth. The symbolism of the poems, Culler says, falls into three categories, which correspond to geographical regions: "the Forest Glade, the Burning or Darkling Plain, and the Wide-Glimmering Sea." An alternative symbol for the Forest Glade is the undersea world, as in "The Forsaken Merman," while the "City of God or Throne of Truth" is sometimes used in place of the Wide-Glimmering Sea. The regions are related either to historical periods or life stages. The first generally symbolizes joy, innocence, and harmony with nature; the second a period of suffering, conflict, and alienation from a hostile environment; "and the third a period of peace in which suffering subsides into calm and then grows up into a new joy, the joy of active service in the world." As Culler points out, these stages are related to the common nineteenth-century cyclic interpretation of history. To apply an Hegelian structure for Arnold's time might produce "the thesis of Romanticism, the antithesis of utilitarianism, and the synthesis of Christian humanism."[1]

Professor Culler's creative and sustained exposition of Arnold's myth does not in any way conflict with the view of Arnold articulated by Lionel Trilling thirty years ago. There is a movement from subjective aestheticism, the private and alienated expression of an introspective dandy who anonymously signed his work "A," to the

1. *Imaginative Reason: The Poetry of Matthew Arnold* (New Haven, Yale University Press, 1966), 4–6. Hereafter cited as Culler.

objective reformer in the market place who essayed to "see things as in themselves they really are" and to lead · others to the "City of God" by offering them a "criticism of life."

From a biographical point of view this analysis is unexceptionable. But when we apply it to Arnold's poetry, we are left with a certain imbalance in the energy and creativity expended on the three symbolic patterns: the third phase is not always reached in Arnold's best poetry. "Dover Beach," for example, closes with the tragic and reverberating "We are here as on a darkling plain." When the third stage is attained, it usually has a flat and almost gratuitous character. Again, if we apply the three stages chronologically to Arnold's poetic career, we find, as Trilling demonstrated years ago, that the significant poetry is almost all a product of the first two stages, that age, experience, and conformity to the demands of responsible and civilized life dried up Arnold's creativity. As he himself wrote in "The Progress of Poesy,"

> Youth rambles on life's arid mount,
> And strikes the rock, and finds the vein,
> And brings the water from the fount,
> The fount which shall not flow again.
>
> The man mature with labour chops
> For the bright stream a channel grand,
> And sees not that the sacred drops
> Ran off and vanish'd out of hand.
>
> And then the old man totters nigh,
> And feebly rakes among the stones.
> The mount is mute, the channel dry;
> And down he lays his weary bones.[2]

2. All quotations from Arnold's poetry are from *The Poetical Works of Matthew Arnold*, C.B. Tinker and H.F. Lowry, eds. (London, Oxford University Press, 1950).

The final "synthesis of Christian humanism" is not reached with equanimity—despite the urbane assurances of Arnold's later criticism, his production of unsuccessful formalist poems like *Balder Dead* or *Merope*, or acts of filial piety like "Rugby Chapel."[3] It is difficult to avoid seeing Arnold as a man with a major talent who, by and large, felt compelled to abandon his own practice of poetry at some time near his thirty-first year. Why he did so was, as much as any other matter, the subject of Trilling's classic account. An attempt to understand the poetic means by which he paradoxically did so will be central to this study.

Although it is commonly said that Arnold was an alienated modern, rendered desolate and paralyzed by his inability to maintain a Christian belief in God or a romantic faith in nature, this description, true as it is, is only symptomatic of an even more fundamental dilemma. It is hard to believe that the son of the liberal and intellectual Dr. Arnold, the progressive antagonist of Newman, could have been paralyzed by the discovery that the Bible and orthodox Christian dogma were not scientifically true. Indeed, we know that he was not. As his brother Tom wrote, Matthew, after his father's death in 1842, "plunged his spirit very deeply . . . in the vast sea of Goethe's art and Spinoza's mysticism. He had already in 1845 drifted far away from Orthodox Christianity, so that the appearance of the translation of Strauss's 'Leben Jesu' in that year [actually 1846]—an epoch-making book for many—found him incurious and uninterested."[4] And this, we remind ourselves, was three years before the publication of Arnold's first volume of poetry. Again, Arnold's early pose as urbane dandy is as foreign to the nature worship of Wordsworth or the early Coleridge as it is to the moralistic world of Dr. Arnold's Rugby. Is it

3. See Clyde de L. Ryals, "Arnold's 'Balder Dead,'" *VP*, 4 (Spring 1966), 67–81, for a contrary opinion.
4. *Manchester Guardian* (May 18, 1888), 8, quoted in Culler, 93.

possible that the "Sea of Faith," whose retreat Arnold memorializes with such anguish, might refer to something more than religious faith? Could the loss of faith indicated in "Dover Beach" and "Stanzas from the Grande Chartreuse" and the passing of the romantic movement, which Arnold mourns in "Memorial Verses," be symbolic and symptomatic of another problem?

I believe that they are. I believe that Arnold, more than any other "modern" poet, was torn by the epistemological and linguistic dilemma that had so concerned the romantics. Arnold, I intend to show, was in his career as a poet profoundly concerned with the possibilities of poetry as a mode of knowing; like Byron, however, he was ultimately too much in sympathy with eighteenth-century aesthetics fully to accept it as such. Although Arnold's poetry does present, over all, a myth, the ironic *meaning* of the myth is that mythic categories are illusory, are what he later designated by Goethe's word, *Aberglaube*. Arnold's problem, thus, is not simply the loss of religious faith or of an organic principle of order in society, but it is a basic and shattering disillusionment with the creative and formative power of human beings, especially as that power is employed in the poet's use of imaginative language.[5] It is not surprising that his attention should, by the 1860s, be turned to seeing things as in themselves they really are, in opposition to seeing them through what was to him the mere subjectivism of modern poetry. It is also not surprising that Arnold's critical interest in the great romantics, both in his poetry and his prose criticism, should reflect no careful reading of Coleridge.

My own strategy in chronicling Arnold's progressive loss of faith in poetry will be to focus most sharply on the

5. See William A. Madden, *Matthew Arnold: A Study of the Aesthetic Temperament in Victorian England* (Bloomington, Indiana University Press, 1967), for an analogous discussion of the conflict between Arnold's "highly developed aesthetic consciousness" and the "countervailing ethical and intellectual currents of his generation."

sea poetry, the creation of which chronologically sur-
rounds his decision of 1848–1851 to turn his energy from
introspective myth-making to school inspection and to
turn from Marguerite to Frances Wightman. The specific poems that formulate symbolically this decision are
"The Forsaken Merman," "The Neckan," the Switzerland poems, "A Summer Night," "Dover Beach," and
"Tristram and Iseult." But in order to see these key
poems in the context of Arnold's entire poetic career, it
will be necessary first to examine briefly the conflicting
forces of his dilemma as they began to polarize in a few
other characteristic poems: "The Strayed Reveller,"
"Resignation," and "Empedocles on Etna."

VARIETIES OF POETIC VISION

A great proportion of Arnold's best poems are concerned with a mythic exploration of the problem of meaning in poetic vision. The question, which he presented in
symbolic terms, might be phrased as follows: How does
the poet relate himself to the external world; how does he
perceive the world objectively and yet retain his own
integrity and individuality? The title poem of his first
volume is devoted to this question. In "The Strayed Reveller," a youth has wandered from the Bacchic revels to
the Palace of Circe where he drinks Circe's enchanted
wine. When Ulysses, another visitor at the palace, suggests that the youth may be the follower of "some divine
bard" and has "learn'd his songs," the youth responds
with a long statement in which he describes three modes
of vision: that of the Gods, that of the "wise bards," and
finally his own. The vision of the Gods is happy, though
superficial. With their "shining eyes" they see below
them a succession of scenes idyllically represented:
Tiresias, the Centaurs, the Indian "drifting" on a cool
lake, the Scythian "on the wide stepp," a ferry on the
"lone Chorasmian stream," and the Heroes "At sunset
nearing / The Happy Islands." These beautifully sculp-

tured and serene forms the poets see, too, the youth explains, but at the cost of experiencing the pain hidden within the forms. He then describes the same scenes through the eyes of the wise bards. Their vision probes beneath the bright surface to reveal the pain and conflict implicit in the human condition and life in time. Not only does the poet perceive the pain, but he suffers it as well

> —such a price
> The Gods exact for song:
> To become what we sing.

The poets not only see the Heroes, as do the Gods,

> —but they share
> Their lives, and former violent toil in Thebes,
> Seven-gated Thebes, or Troy;
> Or where the echoing oars
> Of Argo first
> Startled the unknown sea.

The conflict between the first two modes of vision is fundamental to the function of poetry in the modern world. Can the poet see the world as it really is without becoming subjectively involved in it? On the other hand, is not the beautiful, static, and Apollonian vision of the detached gods illusory? And is not the tortured, empathic, and time-bound vision of the poet too emotional, too subjective, and too short of universal to be valid art? The two kinds of poetry were very much on Arnold's mind at this time, as Culler points out in his perceptive and thorough treatment of "The Strayed Reveller."[6] The two approaches are implied in Arnold's criticism of Clough: "To solve the Universe as you try to do is as

6. Culler, 68–79. See Warren D. Anderson, *Matthew Arnold and the Classical Tradition* (Ann Arbor, The University of Michigan Press, 1965), 24–31, for a discussion of the classical background of "The Strayed Reveller."

irritating as Tennyson's dawdling with its painted shell is fatiguing to me to witness." Similarly, he accuses Clough of being "a mere d——d depth hunter in poetry," of "trying to go into and to the bottom of an object instead of grouping objects."[7] The two visions in "The Strayed Reveller" are especially distressing because they do not present a simple dichotomy between subjective and objective art in the classic Victorian formula. Instead, they represent an insoluble four-way fragmentation of perception. The Apollonian vision of the gods is harmonious, lovely, and objective. But, paradoxically, its objectivity is possible only because it is removed from the flux of life, quiescent and fixed in an imaginative stasis reminiscent of the figures on Keats's Grecian urn. The objective vision in the poem is, therefore, only aesthetic. Because it is removed from time, it is really *only* a creation of the observer, and thus illusory and separated from the existential reality Arnold, as Victorian, was coming increasingly to value. The vision of the wise bards, on the other hand, attempts to deal with reality, with life beneath the polished surface of appearance, with life subject to time, but in so doing it becomes a subjective and vicarious representation, prey to emotional distortion, and far removed from the transcendent ideal of seeing life steadily and whole or the Victorian moral ideal of unimpassioned and objective scientific observation.

In this early pairing of two kinds of poetic vision, here resembling the Apollonian and the Dionysian, Arnold produced an analogue to the conflict he tried to dispel in the 1853 Preface. His unsatisfactory attempt to resolve the difficult paradoxes of "The Strayed Reveller" anticipates his ultimate doubts about poetry itself: the third vision, that of the youth, which Arnold apparently intended as a mediating synthesis between the two extremes, is highly ambiguous and almost perfunctory. Al-

7. *Letters of Matthew Arnold to Arthur Hugh Clough,* H.F. Lowry, ed. (New York, Oxford University Press, 1932), 63, 81, and 99.

though the first two alternatives take up one hundred and
thirty lines, the third—the vision of the youth—requires
only eleven.

> But I, Ulysses,
> Sitting on the warm steps,
> Looking over the valley,
> All day long, have seen,
> Without pain, without labour,
> Sometimes a wild-hair'd Maenad—
> Sometimes a Faun with torches—
> And sometimes, for a moment,
> Passing through the dark stems
> Flowing-robed, the beloved,
> The desired, the divine,
> Beloved Iacchus.

The absence of pain from the youth's vision is attributed
to the enchanted wine of Circe; he closes the poem with
the invocation that opened it.

> Faster, faster,
> O Circe, Goddess,
> Let the wild, thronging train,
> The bright procession
> Of eddying forms,
> Sweep through my soul!

A poetic vision without pain is possible, then—in this
instance through the passivity of a still innocent youth
and the effects on him of Circe's wine. It is difficult,
however, to see how the youth's vision differs significantly
from that of the gods, except for the somewhat gratuitous
introduction of intoxication. In the face of a seemingly
insoluble dilemma, Arnold retreats toward a passive
receptivity in which the "eddying forms, / Sweep
through my soul!"—free of the necessity of subjective
creation. This solution was to be only partially satisfactory
to him, although he suggested similar solutions in poems
like "Mycerinus" and "The Scholar-Gipsy."

"Resignation," as its title implies, explores further

the function of passivity both for poetry and for life. The poem purports to be a dialogue between Arnold and his sister, who is here given the name Fausta because of her impatience at time and human limitation. In response to Fausta's restlessness Arnold suggests the adoption of a stoic resignation as the best means of meeting life and conquering fate. He uses two examples for clarification; the first is a band of gipsies, whom one might expect to be disturbed by the effects of changing times.

> But no!—they rubb'd through yesterday
> In their hereditary way,
> And they will rub through, if they can,
> To-morrow on the self-same plan,
> Till death arrive to supersede,
> For them, vicissitude and need.

The second example is the poet, who, though he feels the changes more deeply and understands them more clearly, must also be detached.

> Though he move mountains, though his day
> Be pass'd on the proud heights of sway,
> Though he hath loosed a thousand chains,
> Though he hath borne immortal pains,
> Action and suffering though he know—
> He hath not lived, if he lives so.

Although Arnold's expression here is awkward, he apparently means that the poet is not to be personally involved in "action and suffering," that is, moving mountains or bearing immortal pains. Like the youth of "The Strayed Reveller," the poet must find a means of seeing that does not involve him subjectively in the pain of life and in the continual changes caused by the passage of time. Instead of the probing, if involuntary, perception of the reveller, the poet in "Resignation" expresses a stoic view of an impersonal general life, unperturbed by human energies and passions and characterized, not by the active joy of the romantics, but by peace.

Before him he sees life unroll,
A placid and continuous whole—
That general life, which does not cease,
Whose secret is not joy, but peace;
That life, whose dumb wish is not miss'd
If birth proceeds, if things subsist;
The life of plants, and stones, and rain,
The life he craves—if not in vain
Fate gave, what chance shall not control,
His sad lucidity of soul.

Culler has rightly said that "Resignation" is "a kind of inverted Tintern Abbey."[8] Arnold's view of nature, which seems "to bear rather than rejoice," is a Victorian shift from Wordsworthian optimism, but again I would say that the shift is more profound than a mere change in attitude toward external nature. The shift is deeply significant because it represents a fundamental change in the theory of the poet's function. In Wordsworth that function was animated by belief in the primacy of the creative imagination, but here it proceeds from a "sad lucidity of soul."

The most significant formulation of Arnold's doubts about poetry, outside of the sea poems—which I am about to discuss—is "Empedocles on Etna." As a number of critics have suggested, "Empedocles" concerns a struggle among three ways of looking at the world—that of Callicles, that of Pausanias, and that of Empedocles. Callicles, whose name is derived from the Greek word for beauty, is an artist who, untroubled by the world around him, sings the songs of a timeless realm of myth. Pausanias is a physician who lives in the city, is concerned about the changes time is working, and is anxious to learn the "spell" by which Empedocles had brought to life a woman seemingly dead. In the apposition of these two characters we recognize a modified version of the conflicts in "The Strayed Reveller." Callicles, as he states in

8. Culler, 38.

35

the opening lines of the play, is a strayed reveller. His art is beautiful, serene, and detached, as his frequent references to Apollo are intended to indicate. He sees as do the gods of the earlier poem; he refuses to admit that the revived woman's condition was genuine death, or that there is any reason for the sophists or "the times" to vex Empedocles. Ironically, it is his singing that urges Empedocles to his death. Pausanias, on the other hand, is involved in the life of his times, is worried about Empedocles' condition, and is eager to learn the secret of miraculous healing. It is not difficult to relate these two characters to their Victorian counterparts or to different elements in the personality of Empedocles. He has been both a poet and a physician. He has attempted to come to grips with reality by means of both art and action, but he is becoming disillusioned by his failures. Arnold's notes on his character are revealing:

> He sees things as they are—the world as it is—God as he is in their stern simplicity.
>
> The sight is a severe and mind-tasking one: to know the mysteries which are communicated to others by fragments, in parables.[9]

In this shorthand description lies the crux of the drama. Man, both in the character of poet and as man of affairs, has been carried beyond the world of parables. If we see in Empedocles a symbol for the mid-Victorian poet and intellectual, we see that the seed of John Locke has borne bitter fruit. Poetry, when it fails to copy external reality accurately, is illusory and childish. When it succeeds, it not only provides a vision of "stern simplicity," but it begets a nearly pathological subjective response, as in Empedocles or the wise bards. Man's inability to make meaningful contact—verbal, mythic, or symbolic—with his world thus forces him to the bare

9. Quoted in *Victorian Poetry and Poetics*, Walter E. Houghton and G. Robert Stange, eds. (Boston, Houghton Mifflin Company, 1959), 412.

peak alone, with no companion at his end. And here the
air is thin indeed.

> He hears nothing but the cry of the torrents,
> And the beating of his own heart.
> The air is thin, the veins swell,
> The temples tighten and throb there—
> Air! air!

Although Empedocles regards banishment to this rarefied
atmosphere as the curse of the isolated artist, it seems
obvious that his exile is the result, not so much of the
artist's isolation in a physical sense, but of loss of faith in
the creative and validly communicative possibilities of
art.

The plot, such as it is, of "Empedocles" substanti-
ates this interpretation. Scene II, which takes place in "A
Glen on the highest skirts of the woody region of Etna,"
brings the three life styles—which may also be regarded
as alternative aspects of Empedocles' personality—into
sharp juxtaposition. Pausanias asks Empedocles to give
him the secret of his healing spell, for

> when the Gods
> Visit us as they do with sign and plague,
> To know those spells of thine which stay their hand
> Were to live free from terror.

Empedocles rebukes the physician for expressing his
desire for immediate solutions to practical problems
(what Carlyle might call "nostrums" or Arnold himself in
later life would call "liberal machinery") and counsels
him to have faith in "mind." Using Empedocles as example, Pausanias responds with the suspicion of the Victorian man of action: "Mind is a light which the Gods
mock us with, / To lead those false who trust it." At this
point the sound of Callicles' harp rises from below with
its ironic mythic representation of the Centaur teaching
Achilles how to live like a hero. Empedocles then delivers
a lecture, intended as a response both to Pausanias' practi-
cality and to Callicles' aestheticism.

This lecture, three hundred and fifty lines long, has not been a favorite of the critics. Its turgid and awkward didacticism is rightly felt to be a discordant note in a classic drama. Surely, Arnold too, as highly as he valued the lecture as a criticism of life, must have considered it as a jarring intrusion. But this jarring intrusion is the point of the poem. It dramatizes painfully the unhappy quandary of Empedocles: He "sees things as they are" but is unable to accept the human creation of poetry as a valid mode of knowing or to view human action as a useful mode of living. The epistemological basis for this rejection appears in the first two stanzas of Empedocles' speech.

> The out-spread world to span
> A cord the Gods first slung,
> And then the soul of man
> There, like a mirror, hung,
> And bade the winds through space impel the gusty toy.

> Hither and thither spins
> The wind-borne, mirroring soul,
> A thousand glimpses wins,
> And never sees a whole;
> Looks once, and drives elsewhere, and leaves its last employ.

The modern truncation of self, word, thing, and reality, with its accompanying mirror aesthetic, is the fundamental assumption underlying Empedocles' horror. In one sense he—and I believe we may read *Arnold* here—is a "negative romantic."[10] Like Byron, he can accept only the externalist, passive way of knowing, but he has lost faith in the beneficence of the objective nature that is thus known. If "Resignation" is an inverted "Tintern

10. Negative romanticism, according to Morse Peckham, is expressed by a man "who has left static mechanism but has not yet arrived at a reintegration of his thought and art in terms of dynamic organicism," in "Toward a Theory of Romanticism," *PMLA*, 66 (March 1951), 15.

Abbey," Empedocles' speech may be considered an inverted "Essay on Man," a mirror held to nature as was
Pope's, but a mirror held to a nature no longer conceived
as the construction of a benevolent Creator.

> Man errs not that he deems
> His welfare his true aim,
> He errs because he dreams
> The world does but exist that welfare to bestow.

When Empedocles compares the confused reflections of
the mirror to the traditional human conception of God,
he concludes that God, in this reflection, is simply an
illusory subjective creation introduced as a therapeutic
fantasy to ease the horror of human failure.

> But, next, we would reverse
> The scheme ourselves have spun,
> And what we made to curse
> We now would lean upon,
> And feign kind Gods who perfect what man vainly tries.

Man's passivity and his dependence on the forces of external reality are Empedocles' theme: "Born into life we
are, and life must be our mould." He closes his stoic
teaching by counseling Pausanias to forget his subjective
questioning of "Heaven and Fate" and to live bravely and
rationally without illusion. "Because thou must not
dream, thou need'st not then despair!" Ironically, this
advice, in its flat gratuitousness so similar to the conclusion of many of Arnold's poems, is advice that Empedocles is unable himself to follow.

At the conclusion of Empedocles' oration, another
song of Callicles begins what is to become an increasingly
unbearable tension between Empedocles' withdrawn stoi-
cism and Callicles' world of myth. It is this confrontation
that brings about the final catastrophe. The three myths
that Callicles sings for Empedocles are of cumulatively
painful significance for him. First, he hears the tale of
Cadmus and Harmonia; their transformation, in which
"Placed safely in changed forms, the pair / Wholly forget

their first sad life," is an ironic commentary on his own growing paralysis. For Empedocles, the story of the metamorphosis of Cadmus and Harmonia is not only a proof of the generally illusory nature of poetry, but also a suggestion that dehumanization is a defense against the pain of human life.

The next song, the myth of the Titan Typho's hopeless struggle with Zeus, comes at the beginning of Act II, after Pausanias has descended the mountain, leaving Empedocles alone at the summit. For Typho, Callicles sings, the sound of the harp is unbearable because it recalls the pain of his defeat and punishment by Zeus. This song is in fact a recapitulation of the first two modes of aesthetic vision of "The Strayed Reveller." Typho's writhing in helpless pain at the consciousness of injustice corresponds to the suffering of the bards in that poem. The gods in "Empedocles," as in "The Strayed Reveller," listen with serene and unimpassioned pleasure.

> And the white Olympus-peaks
> Rosily brighten, and the soothed Gods smile
> At one another from their golden chairs,
> And no one round the charmed circle speaks.

Here, however, is no gratuitous third possibility, no "help for pain." The lesson Empedocles learns from the song is that action in life is futile:

> The brave, impetuous heart yields everywhere
> To the subtle, contriving head;

art is not relevant to real life, and it is at best an elegant amusement for the dwellers on Mount Olympus.

The final myth, which drives Empedocles to suicide, is significantly that of the musical contest between Marsyas and Apollo. Upon defeating Marsyas, Apollo coldly orders him to be flayed alive. And here, for Empedocles, is the final proof that poetry has no relevance to real life. Apollo's indifference to the suffering Faun leaves Empedocles finally alone and helpless in a meaningless and empty universe.

With the loss of faith in myth and symbol as means of knowing the world not only does Empedocles lose "joy" but the external world shrinks to a pale abstraction. The stars, for instance, "once lived," once

> moved joyfully
> Among august companions,
> In an older world, peopled by Gods,
> In a mightier order,
> The radiant, rejoicing, intelligent Sons of Heaven.
> But now, ye kindle
> Your lonely, cold-shining lights
> Unwilling lingerers
> In the heavenly wilderness. . . .

Empedocles is now imprisoned in the cave of his self-hood, William Blake's Ulro. He is, as he says, "A living man no more. . . . / Nothing but a devouring flame of thought— / But a naked, eternally restless mind!" In a desperate attempt to regain a moment's freedom, "Not to die wholly, not to be all enslaved," to make some contact with reality, Empedocles plunges into the crater.

The closing song of Callicles is apparently intended to balance the violence of Empedocles' act and to complete a tragic purging. If the song fails of this intent, it is nonetheless significant, perhaps in ways of which Arnold was unaware. Callicles declares that the summit of Etna, witness of this human suffering, is unsuitable for Apollo and the Muses to visit:

> Not here, O Apollo!
> Are haunts meet for thee.

Apollo cares no more for Empedocles than he did for Marsyas. Apollo and his choir are safely insulated from human anguish, in Helicon or Olympus, "their endless abode." Their song is timeless, generalized, and serene:

> What will be for ever;
> What was from of old.

41

First hymn they the Father
Of all things; and then,
The rest of immortals,
The action of men.

The day in his hotness,
The strife with the palm;
The night in her silence,
The stars in their calm.

The implicit meaning of "Empedocles on Etna," though reached with more suffering and considerably more talent, is very much like the belief of Poe: Truth and poetry are like oil and water. In many ways, "Empedocles" is Arnold's most complete poetic presentation of his attitudes toward poetry; it leads naturally to the 1853 Preface. But even more revealing, in terms of Arnold's art and personality, are the sea poems and the Switzerland poems, which dramatize so beautifully the process by which Arnold reached the bare peak of Etna.

MARGUERITE AND THE METAMORPHOSIS OF A MERMAN

In his account of Dante's art in *The Figure of Beatrice*, Charles Williams describes Dante's aesthetic theory as the "affirmation of images." The central image of almost all of his poetry and especially of *The Divine Comedy*, the image—the term *figura* is apt here—through which all comes to be known is an image of romantic love: a young girl whom Dante did not marry, but whom he loved throughout his life—Beatrice. I should like to suggest an analogy to the life and poetry of Matthew Arnold. Arnold's best poems, "The Forsaken Merman," "The Neckan," "A Summer Night," "The Buried Life," the Switzerland series, "Dover Beach," and "Tristram and Iseult" are "known" through the image of a French girl named Marguerite, whom Arnold loved but did not marry. Arnold's confidence in Marguerite is a paradigm of his faith in the images of poetry; his ultimate loss of faith in the image of the girl paralleled his disillusionment with poetry as a way of coming to know reality. It is not necessary to assert categorically the actual existence of Marguerite, but I do believe in it. Although there is no conclusive evidence of Marguerite's existence, many students of Arnold have accepted her actuality since the publication of his correspondence with Clough and its apparent references to her. Especially interesting has been Park Honan's very recent report on Arnold's "romantic passion" for Mary Claude, who may have been a model for Marguerite.[11] In any case, Marguerite as a powerful and important symbol in Arnold's emotional and imaginative life surely does exist, and this influence is what particularly concerns us.

W. Stacy Johnson has remarked that "the virtue of Arnold's poetry . . . consists in the degree of steadiness and wholeness, to use his language, and of adequacy to serious human experience which is achieved in a series of poems, including 'Dover Beach,' 'The Forsaken Merman,' 'Tristram and Iseult.' "[12] I agree with Johnson's high estimate of the centrality of these poems in Arnold's work, but I intend to go a step beyond his perceptive close readings of them—particularly in the direction of relating them to the poems I have just named and to Arnold's career as a whole.

I propose first to analyze "The Forsaken Merman" from a vantage point somewhat different from Johnson's[13] and to consider along with it its companion piece "The Neckan" (including the latter poem's revealing alterations). I should then like in a fresh way to connect the two merman poems with the often discussed biographical crisis expressed in the Marguerite

11. "A Note on Matthew Arnold in Love," *VNL* (Spring 1971), 11–15.
12. *The Voices of Matthew Arnold: An Essay in Criticism* (New Haven, Yale University Press, 1961), 38.
13. *Voices*, 84–90.

poems, "A Summer Night," "The Buried Life," and the unhappy resolution of the crisis, partially reflected in "Dover Beach" and "Tristram and Iseult." I hope to show how Arnold, through his developing creation of a myth of the sea and of Marguerite, chronicled the dialogue of his own mind with itself and arrived at an inwardly troubled but outwardly powerful and influential conclusion about art.

*   *   *   *

Arnold's sources for "The Forsaken Merman" and his alterations of them serve to reveal much of his approach to the story. Tinker and Lowry suggest that Arnold may have used either George Borrow's translation of the Danish ballad, "The Deceived Merman," or his prose account of the story in a review of Just Mathias Thiele's *Danske Folkesagn*.[14] In the Danish originals the point of view is that of the land-dwelling human beings as opposed to that of the nonhuman inhabitants of the sea. The story is not about a merman; it is about a human being, Grethe or Agnes, as she is variously called; it expresses little sympathy for the merman or his children. At the conclusion of the prose account we are told that "Grethe ever after stayed with her parents, and let the merman himself take care of his ugly little children"; in Borrow's translation of the ballad, the merman (who is described as a fair demon with yellow eyes and a green beard) begs the girl to consider the children:

> Think on them, Agnes, think on them all;
> Think on the great one, think on the small.

Her answer to her supernatural lover is calmly unsympathetic:

14. *The Poetry of Matthew Arnold, a Commentary* (New York, Oxford University Press, 1940), 130–32. Hereafter cited as *Commentary*.

Little, O little care I for them all,
Or for the great one, or for the small.[15]

As in so much poetry of the Victorian age, the age
of the dramatic monologue, point of view in "The Forsaken Merman" is revealing. In opposition to his immediate sources and to many of the less immediate analogues
in the myths of Beauty and the Beast and of Cupid and
Psyche, Arnold has shifted the sympathies of the reader
from his fellow human being to an alien creature—from
the familiar beauty to the unknown beast. The shift in
point of view accomplishes two things: first, it increases
our sympathy with the pathos of the merman's hopeless
plight; second, it increases the guilt associated with Margaret's faithlessness. Later on I shall suggest some reasons
for Arnold's shift from the conventional emphasis.

The most powerful reversal of the values of Arnold's
sources is not in point of view, however, but in the careful
precision of the imagery he uses to develop the fundamental land–sea conflict in the poem. Arnold creates a
sharp contrast between the merman's free and colorful
water-world and Margaret's walled and achromatous village. He distinguishes the red gold throne in the heart of
the sea vividly from the "white-wall'd town, / And the
little grey church on the windy shore." He sets the freedom of the sea folk and their "wild white horses" in the
boundless infinities of the ocean against the rigidities of
life behind the walls that compress the village, the "narrow paved streets" within those walls, and the "small
leaded panes" of the church. The merman and his children must peer through narrow windows to see Margaret
—who is sitting close to a pillar—because "shut stands
the door." In order to see through the windows, they
must stand on gravestones. Similarly, the emotional satis-
factions and freedoms of the sea as evidenced in the
children and symbolized in the more direct eroticism of
the coiling and twining sea-snakes are in opposition to the

15. *Commentary*, 132.

chilly sexlessness of the town where even the mother and father of Arnold's sources are replaced by mere kinsfolk, who are praying in the church.[16] Despite the erotic and generative freedom of the sea in comparison to the inflexibility of the land, Arnold does not, as one might suppose, find the moral aspects of the land superior to those of the sea. Although Margaret sat on a red gold throne, "the youngest sate on her knee," and "She comb'd its bright hair, and she tended it well." Yet when the merman calls and the "little ones moan" outside the church, Margaret refuses to answer them:

> But, ah, she gave me never a look
> For her eyes were seal'd to the holy book!
> Loud prays the priest; shut stands the door.

Perhaps the most striking contrast is the peaceful tranquility of life in the sea as opposed to the ceaseless activity of the land. The merman and his family dwell in

> Sand-strewn caverns, cool and deep,
> Where the winds are all asleep;
> Where the spent lights quiver and gleam.

They live secure from the world in an abode of meditative silence; they have achieved that state which Arnold later called "disinterestedness," not by being above the fitful tempests of practical life, but by being below them. Their serenity is achieved, not by a detached godlike overview from above, as in "The Strayed Reveller," but by an inner relation to a creative "buried life." Life in the town, in contrast, is characterized by constant movement—if not "sick hurry." Arnold's skillful employment of present participles increases the impression of incessant and mechanical activity. The town is "humming," the spinning wheel is "whizzing," Margaret is "singing."

16. It is interesting to speculate on how much of Arnold's imagery in "The Forsaken Merman" was suggested by Tennyson's "The Mermaid" and "The Merman." The similarity was noted by the reviewer of the 1849 volume for *Fraser's Magazine*, 39 (May 1849), 576.

For the humming street, and the child with its toy!
For the priest, and the bell, and the holy well;
For the wheel where I spun,
And the blessed light of the sun!

Even the need for prayer, which had drawn Margaret from the depths, is here satisfied by a mechanical and formalized "murmur of folk at their prayers." Arnold's opposition of sea and land suggests more, however, than a dichotomy between action and inaction or even an Arnoldian dialectic of disinterestedness opposed to the Philistine world of "practice." The depths are not only a peaceful retreat; they contain the fundamental mysteries of the universe. For "ranged all round" the deep caverns are those primal forces of nature, the sea-beasts and sea-snakes, identified by Tennyson in "The Mermaid" and "The Kraken" with the final mysteries of sex, life, and the internal energies of artistic creation. Here the sea people witness a reality undreamed of by the surface-bound townsfolk as the "great whales come sailing by," their eyes ever open in their unceasing circumnavigation of the world. The cool, dark caverns assume, then, the profoundly revelatory function of the underground or under-sea experience characteristic of myths and dreams. In the town there is a monotonous and sterile whirring, whizzing, humming, murmuring, and praying behind walls and shut doors and among gravestones. In the sea there is color, imagination, life, love, and the hidden meaning of the world.

But what, we may now ask, does all of this mean? The answer is complex, but worth the effort of untangling. Johnson has read the conflict between the sea and the "human land" as "associated . . . with the conflict between the isolated natural self and the social or moral self."[17] Arnold, in this interpretation, has used Easter, the time of resurrection, to add meaning to Margaret's rising from the "grave-like, womb-like caverns of the sea" and to her return from "natural to human life." Her

17. *Voices*, 84.

triumph over nature, however, brings pain and suffering. "If she has gained her soul, which she was in danger of losing with the merman, she has lost her love, her natural delights: in a certain sense she has had to lose her life in order to find it. This is Easter from the point of view of the depths."[18]

The chief difficulty with this interpretation, it seems to me, is that this is not "Easter from the point of view of the depths"; it is Easter from the point of view of Margaret. It assumes that the story is more about Margaret than it is about the merman. Yet it is clear that Arnold manipulated his sources to place the merman and his anguish at the center of the poem. Although Johnson suggests that "Arnold does imaginatively join the two even as he reveals them in conflict," the theme of the poem in this reading still contrasts "the way of the animal" to the "moral way."[19]

Arnold's imagery, I believe, shows us something quite different from a simple conflict between natural instincts and human or religious moral standards. Arnold's shift in point of view from that of his sources and his carefully controlled development of imagery created, instead of a simple conflict between erotic love and moral duty, a poem complex in meaning and profoundly ironic. Superficially, Arnold took what is traditionally amoral, alien, and irresponsible (a merman) and contrasted him to what is traditionally moral, familiar, and faithful (the everyday life of conventionally religious human beings in a small town). In the poem, Arnold reverses the qualities of each. The sea, in Arnold's poem, represents freedom, beauty, love, and the creative energies of life, yet paradoxically it also represents moral responsibility to others, as in the care of children. The land represents imprisonment by convention, insensitivity to the deepest moral values, and monotonous, mechanical, incessant activity. Margaret's failure to respond to the beauty of the sea

18. *Voices*, 87.
19. *Voices*, 89.

world, "the sea of faith" as Arnold was to call it in "Dover Beach," does *not* result in her losing her life to gain it; instead, it chronicles her tragic refusal to give herself completely to the deepest experiences of life. For Margaret, Easter is not a symbolic resurrection from death to life; it is merely a legal observance to save herself, according to orthodox belief. Easter marks Margaret's failure to accept real life; she is reborn, not into life, but into spiritual death. Through an exquisite irony Arnold shows that her choice of conventional morality and her timorous rejection of the depths of being cause her to commit the most shocking immorality, the Judas sin— treachery.

The application of "The Forsaken Merman" to the problem of artistic perception and creation, which we discussed in relationship to "The Strayed Reveller," "Resignation," and "Empedocles," seems plain. The dilemma in "The Strayed Reveller" developed from the position that beauty and harmony come only from a divine and detached overview of the world. Art must be removed from life: Apollo's rightful place is Helicon, not Etna, as we learn in "Empedocles." "Resignation" tells us "the poet sees not deep, but wide." All of these statements suggest a mirror theory of art (almost impossible to realize because of the flaws in human mirrors). In "The Forsaken Merman," however, beauty and harmony are created in the depths. The subjective engagement of the wise bards and the objective aesthetic view of the gods are imaginatively fused in a poetic myth of poignant loveliness. Beauty stems from the buried life rather than from the Olympian overview.

Another important poem of Arnold makes a similar attempt at formulating a creative and inner theory of art: "The Buried Life." Although it is not a sea poem, it has often been related to the Marguerite group. The theme, like the conclusion of "The Forsaken Merman," is the impossibility of meaningful dialogue between lovers in their flow of "mocking words." Yet, beneath human "disguises," the speaker of the poem muses, there runs

:hrough the deep recesses of our breast / The unre-
garded river of our life," of which we desire knowledge.
Despite the "stupefying power" of external reality, with
its distractions and its destruction of the integrity of the
individual,

> Yet still, from time to time, vague and forlorn,
> From the soul's subterranean depth upborne
> As from an infinitely distant land,
> Come airs, and floating echoes, and convey
> A melancholy into all our day.

This relation with the buried life may—though rarely—
occur at the tone of voice or the touch of a lover's
hand.

> A bolt is shot back somewhere in our breast,
> And a lost pulse of feeling stirs again.
> The eye sinks inward, and the heart lies plain,
> And what we mean, we say, and what we would, we know.
> A man becomes aware of his life's flow . . .
> And an unwonted calm pervades his breast.
> And then he thinks he knows
> The hills where his life rose,
> And the sea where it goes.

"The Buried Life" is not only a psychological treatment of Arnold's conflict between his deepest and perhaps unconscious desires and the conventions and
demands of the external world—what Freud termed the
"reality principle"—but it is also a poignant analogy to
Arnold's concern with the possibilities of the creative
imagination. As Peckham has written, "The unconscious
is really a postulate to the creative imagination, and as
such continues today without the divine sanction as part
of present-day critical theory. It is that part of the mind
through which novelty enters into the personality and
hence into the world in the form of art and ideas. We
today conceive of the unconscious spatially as inside and
beneath; the earlier romantics conceived of it as outside
and above. We descend into the imagination; they rose

50

into it."[20] Arnold is experimenting with a distinctively modern conception of the imagination. His loss of faith in the romantic transcendental view is reflected in "The Strayed Reveller," where the overview is presented as fixed and static. Only rarely does Arnold's poetry describe the imagination as an inner, buried life, as the poem of that title indicates. This view is damaged by faithlessness in "The Forsaken Merman" and is gradually abandoned in the succeeding poems.

Four years after the publication of "The Forsaken Merman" Arnold published a second poem dealing with a similar theme. Its chief source was undoubtedly Benjamin Thorpe's *Northern Mythology*, and its ballad genre was possibly influenced by Arnold's interest in Heine at the time.[21] This poem, "The Neckan," immediately preceded "The Forsaken Merman" in the 1853 *Poems* and continued to do so in Arnold's subsequent arrangements of his verse. There are really two versions of "The Neckan": one, as it first appeared in 1853; the other, as it appeared in 1869, with two added stanzas that change the meaning considerably. Although it was not published until 1869, the addition may have been written as early as 1854.[22] I shall treat "The Neckan," therefore, as two poems, beginning with the first version.

As the ballad opens, the Neckan (it is almost impossible not to associate him with the merman) is "on the headlands, / The Baltic Sea along." He is sitting with his harp of gold and singing a "plaintive song." On the slope below him are his wife, a human being and a Christian, and his children. As the melancholy of his song indicates, he has not found happiness on the land:

20. "Romanticism," 13.
21. *Northern Mythology* (London, 1851), 75 and 80, Vol. II of *Scandinavian Traditions and Superstitions*. See Kenneth Allott, "Matthew Arnold's 'The Neckan': The Real Issues," *VP*, 2 (Winter 1964), 60–63; and my "The Real Issues in Arnold's 'The Neckan,'" *VP* (Summer 1964), 205–8.
22. See *Commentary*, 127.

> He sings not of the ocean,
>> Its shells and roses pale;
> Of earth, of earth the Neckan sings,
>> He hath no other tale.

His song does not reflect the wonder and beauty of Donne's or Tennyson's mermaids singing, or even the faint hint of reality and life grasped at by J. Alfred Prufrock. The Neckan's song is but "a mournful stave / Of all he saw and felt on earth / Far from the kind sea-wave." The Neckan sings of his wandering on the land as a knight, although "earthly knights have harder hearts / Than the sea-children own." He recounts his wedding on earth and his being driven off, with his bride, when the guests discover his identity. Moved by his wife's desire for a "Christian mate," he returns to the land and seeks to be baptized. A priest, passing him by, declares that

> "Sooner shall this my staff bear leaves,
>> Than thou shalt Heaven behold."

The priest then rides on, leaving the isolated and alien Neckan, like the uprooted children of Israel, weeping by the waters of Babylon:

> The cassock'd priest rode onwards,
>> And vanished with his mule;
> But Neckan in the twilight grey
>> Wept by the river-pool.

Both the point of view in "The Neckan" and the handling of the imagery are similar to those in "The Forsaken Merman." The only colors in the poem are the green of the Baltic, the "roses pale" beneath the ocean, and the gold of the Neckan's harp (one thinks of the harps of the unhappy Tristram and Empedocles). The harp is a luminous reminder of the sea "in the twilight grey," as the black-cassocked priest on his white mule rejects the Neckan's plea for salvation. Once again Arnold has pictured the land's superficial, conventional morality and religiosity, which reject the magical beauty of the sea and the alien Neckan's poignant desire for spiritual rebirth. The Neckan (or merman) has attempted in this poem to follow his "Margaret" (the wife is not named in this poem) to her own environment, since she will not return to his. He rises to earth again "through the billows" so "that Neckan Heaven might gain." Through baptism he hopes to achieve the reconciliation of land and sea necessary for his personal salvation and necessary in restoring his relationship to his loved one, the emotion-laden pivot around which the whole argument revolves. In the first version of the poem, salvation for the strange Neckan is denied by the conventional priest.

Fifteen years later, however, Arnold changed his thoughts about this work; a quite different version appeared in the 1869 edition. Although only two stanzas had been added, the emphasis of the poem had shifted almost to a direct reversal. The first added stanza was inserted immediately after the priest rebukes the Neckan:

"Sooner shall this my staff bear leaves,
     Than thou shalt Heaven behold."

In the first version Arnold followed this stanza with the priest's leaving the rejected Neckan weeping in the twilight. The following stanza appears in the second version:

But, lo, the staff, it budded!
     It green'd, it branch'd, it waved.
"O ruth of God," the priest cried out,
     "This lost sea-creature saved!"

Now, instead of hopeless despair, the sense of alienation and abandonment of "The Forsaken Merman" and of the first version of "The Neckan," we have a note of hope, a promise of salvation. The incident of the budding staff is found not only in Thorpe, but also in the Tann-häuser legend, which Arnold might have found in Swin-burne's "Laus Veneris" if he wrote the stanza as late as 1866. In the Tannhäuser story, the blossoming staff sym-bolizes the possibility of escape from imprisonment in the mountain of Venus. The association of the earlier Margaret of the generative sea-caves and the foam-born Aphrodite is suggestive.

The second stanza that Arnold added in 1869 followed the one in which the priest leaves the Neckan weeping:

> He wept: "The earth hath kindness,
> 　　The sea, the starry poles;
> Earth, sea, and sky, and God above—
> 　　But, ah, not human souls!"

These lines modify and explain the other added stanza. Arnold is saying, I think, that total happiness on the land among conventional human beings is unattainable for the outsider from the sea, from the deep world of the imagination. Human souls, imprisoned as they are by circumstance and custom, have little kindness for the alien values of freedom, faith, love, or even poetic creativity. Yet the man from the sea must attempt to live on the land (must the sensitive Victorian intellectual find his salvation in the crude society of Philistia?), and God and nature will approve, as is evidenced by the budding of the staff. Despite the disbelief of the narrow-minded priest, the "lost sea-creature" is saved—but not in or through society. This pious salvation is as gratuitous as the "God's tremendous voice" of the Marguerite poem, "Meeting," or as so many of Arnold's stoic conclusions.

We have, then, in these three poems—in "The Forsaken Merman" and in the first and second versions of "The Neckan"—a revealing progression in Arnold's thought. In the first poem a merman is abandoned by his human lover, who returns to the land. The merman, unable to persuade the human being to return to the sea, must therefore remain in the sea with his abandoned family to live in hopeless loneliness. In the second poem, the first version of "The Neckan," a merman, to please his disaffected human mate, leaves the ocean for the land and attempts to gain admittance into human society through baptism. He is rejected by the priest and thereby denied the entry he so ardently desires. In the third poem, his attempt to live on land is again met by hostility —he is still an outsider—but his effort brings about a miraculous promise of ultimate salvation; we see him, however, in the last stanza, as in the first, with his family, singing sadly by the edge of the sea.

*   *   *   *

In March of 1849 James Anthony Froude wrote to Clough concerning *The Strayed Reveller* that "there are some things like the Forsaken Merman that sound right out from the heart."[23] The publication of the Marguerite poems three years later in what H. W. Garrod has called "Marguerite's book" would substantiate Froude's intuition.[24] Several critics have speculated that "The Forsaken Merman" is truly part of the Marguerite poems. Garrod, for one, goes so far as to declare that the 1852 volume in which the Marguerite poems first appeared "might better have been called *The Forsaken Merman*, and have taken into itself, from the 1849 volume, both the poem of that title and *The Voice*." P. F. Baum, on the other hand, in his useful summary of the Marguerite problem, dismisses the speculation. Although "there is a Margaret in 'The Forsaken Merman' . . . ," he writes, "all such attempted extensions of the canon are risky and gratuitous."[25]

23. *Letters to Clough*, 27 n.
24. *Poetry and the Criticism of Life* (Cambridge, Harvard University Press, 1931), 36.
25. Ibid., 36; *Ten Studies in the Poetry of Matthew Arnold* (Durham, N.C., Duke University Press, 1958), 83; E.D.H. Johnson, in *The Alien Vision of Victorian Poetry* (Princeton, Princeton University Press, 1952), 161, finds it "impossible not to perceive in ["The Forsaken Merman"] a metaphorical presentation of the poet's hapless passion for the shadowy Marguerite." Edward K. Brown finds a similar connection, in *Matthew Arnold: A Study in Conflict* (Chicago, University of Chicago Press, 1948), 37; while Penelope Fitzgerald, attempting to prove that Arnold wrote "The Forsaken Merman" on

The letters of Arnold to Clough from Switzerland in September of 1848 and September of 1849 indicate some relationship with a French girl, which must have ended at the latest by June of 1851, when he married Frances Wightman. Even if Marguerite remains a shadowy figure, Arnold clearly was involved during the years 1848–1851 with a momentous personal decision, of which the painful process is recorded, in part at least, in the Marguerite poems. The result of Arnold's decision was more than his rejection of Marguerite and his marriage to Frances Wightman. He seems also, as the record of his poems indicates, to have begun to lose faith in poetry as a valid means of cognition. In this period, he relinquished his total commitment to art and assumed the post of Inspector of Schools. Further, he rejected, in his famous Preface of 1853, his earlier subjective poetry—for reasons we shall discuss later—and at the same time initiated his new career as critic. Within four years he was Professor of Poetry at Oxford, in his case an ironic sign that he was himself no longer a productive poet. Keeping in mind what we have learned about the merman poems, we may now turn to the Marguerite poems, which Arnold collected under the heading "Switzerland," and review them in preparation for the remainder of the poems which deal directly with Arnold's decision.

The situation in these poems seems to be that a love affair is breaking up—inevitably, yet through no fault of the participants. The chief responsibility for the failure in love and faith is attributed in the poems to God, or at least to an immutable reality. In "Meeting" the poet springs "to make my choice," but

> Again in tones of ire
> I hear a God's tremendous voice:
> "Be counsell'd, and retire."

---

the Isle of Man, in "Matthew Arnold's Summer Holiday," *English*, 6 (1946), 77–81, denies any connection to Marguerite.

In "Parting" we learn that God granted to "Nature"

> A heart ever new—
> To all always open,
> To all always true.

"A God, a God their severance ruled!" is the pathetic explanation for the inevitable human isolation in "To Marguerite—Continued." The hopeless sense of isolation and alienation caused by God's creation of the estranging "sea of life" is again referred to in the nostalgic "Terrace at Berne":

> Like driftwood spars, which meet and pass
> Upon the boundless ocean-plain,
> So on the sea of life, alas!
> Man meets man—meets, and quits again.

When God is not named as the direct cause of the estrangement, the blame is laid to an inescapable and predetermined "curse of life," as in "Absence," in which Arnold laments that "we forget because we must / And not because we will." In "A Farewell" Arnold seems to say that "the world" renders love and faith difficult, if not impossible:

> But in the world I learnt, what there
> Thou too wilt surely one day prove,
> That will, that energy, though rare,
> Are yet far, far less rare than love.

As the poems and letters to Clough indicate—and as the subsequent course of his life shows clearly—Arnold was reaching a decision to abandon a love affair and a way of life. He was also implying the impossibility of communication in poetry as a parallel to the impossibility of communicating with Marguerite.

> Yes! in the sea of life enisled,
> With echoing straits between us thrown,

Dotting the shoreless watery wild,
We mortal millions live *alone.*

Arnold's preface of the following year reveals that he intended to cease creating the kind of poetry he wrote best. Yet, in these poems there is little evidence of conscious volition on Arnold's part. He has not decided in the poems to stop loving Marguerite; instead, he complains that God has made love impossible. He does not decide to leave Marguerite and return to England; he laments that a God has divided them by an "umplumb'd, salt, estranging sea."

There are two ways to interpret Arnold's fatalism in the poems. We may either regard it as a seriously considered world view, or we may suspect an element of rationalization. We may suspect, as Johnson has said, "that Arnold is indulging in attempts at therapy, comforting himself with dark generalization on his own experience, rather than rendering experience in such a way as to discover its meanings."[26] It is possible to compromise by interpreting the poems in both ways at the same time; certainly, the passivity that is associated with the Lockian theory of knowledge often shifts into fatalism or determinism.

But how does Arnold's "Merman" fit into the Marguerite pattern? "The Forsaken Merman" is essential to the Marguerite canon because it goes so much further than the other poems in revealing Arnold's inner tensions, yet by sea-change transmuting them into the mythic and dramatic. We cannot help suspecting that here, too, Arnold is "indulging in attempts at therapy," but here he is also "rendering experience in such a way as to discover its meanings." He has found a usable objective correlative to change his personal experience into something rich and strange.

If naming the inescapable voice of God as the direct cause of estrangement is partially an elaborate evasion of

26. *Voices,* 52.

personal responsibility for the decision represented by the Marguerite poems, we should reasonably expect to find the same sort of device operating in "The Forsaken Merman." We do, but here the artifice is at once subtler and more generally meaningful. The poem invites an immediate association of Arnold with the merman and of Marguerite with the faithless Margaret. To a point, such an identification is valid—but only to a point. If there was indeed, a real love affair with a flesh-and-blood Marguerite, the situation was similar, with all its emotional, aesthetic, and moral complexities, but the roles of the actors may have been, in part at least, reversed. Although Arnold complains of Marguerite in "Parting" that "To the lips, ah! of others / Those lips have been prest," it is not necessarily Marguerite who deserts Arnold. Although we cannot be sure of the circumstances that brought about the end of the affair, we do know that Arnold left Switzerland, returned to England, and married someone else less than two years after his reference to a girl in 1849. Although Margaret in "The Forsaken Merman" heeds the voice of God and puts the "unplumb'd, salt, estranging sea" between herself and her lover, Arnold himself may have made a similar choice in his personal life. In the "Merman" Margaret leaves the "buried life" of love, faith, and creativity to return to the colorless workaday world of whirring and spinning activity. In fact, of course, Arnold himself left the freedom of Switzerland to return to the land of the Philistines, with its "sick hurry" and the "incessant grind" of the school inspector. It could be said that even in Switzerland Arnold gave up his subjection to Marguerite in favor of nature on the mountaintops, as recorded in "Parting." His rejection of the "unconquer'd joy" of Marguerite for the "vast range of snow" and the "stillness" of the isolated peaks is reminiscent of Empedocles' rejection of Callicles for the peak of Etna. Instead of committing suicide, however, Arnold followed Empedocles' advice rather than his action and stoically returned home to work.

Although Arnold's affair may have been actual, as

some evidence suggests, the psychological and artistic meaning of Marguerite is even more significant if she is entirely Arnold's creation. Whatever Marguerite's status as a living person may have been, we do know that she existed for Arnold as a powerful symbol that had a direct relationship to his career as a poet. The strategy of role reversal in the merman poems allowed Arnold to present in an objective myth the emotional problem of love versus duty, the social and moral problem of private integrity versus public action, and the aesthetic problem of an inner creative art versus a conditioned response to an external world of "given" reality. The role reversal may at the same time have served a therapeutic need for Arnold's troubled personality. Marguerite and the inescapable conventions of the world could conveniently be blamed for a decision that Arnold had himself made. Yet paradoxically, Arnold could retain his self-image as artist and lover by associating himself with the betrayed merman who, through no fault of his own, is compelled to leave the idyllic sea world and live on land. "The Forsaken Merman" presents the story at its crisis and chronicles the "betrayal." The two versions of "The Neckan," which followed, treat the necessary consequence of the merman's removal to the land and, finally, as the priest's staff blossoms, suggest a divine sanction of his choice, similar to those of the Marguerite poems.

It may be argued in opposition to adding the merman poems to the Marguerite canon that Arnold seems to use the sea quite differently in the two groups. If the sea is the source of beauty, love, and faith in "The Forsaken Merman," why is it sometimes (though not always) described as a divisive wasteland in the Marguerite poems, where human beings are "like driftwood spars, which meet and pass / Upon the boundless ocean-plain"? This shift in the use of sea symbolism is in some sense the point of the poems. As Swinburne could on occasion use the sea as an emblem for unconsciousness and womblike passivity, so Arnold here, in accordance with his changing view of the world, has come to regard the once creative sea as an empty emblem of division between persons and of the impossibility of the self's relating to a meaningful reality. He no longer has faith in the unifying and formative power of myth and poetry, as symbolized by the generative ocean depths associated with the ambiguous Marguerite. The point of view has changed. The merman speaks from the point of view of the land. He has made the same choice that the merman's Margaret made, and he yearns toward the sea with the same unhappy sense of loss.

Another reason for the altered use of sea imagery inheres in the rhetorical and symbolic structure of the poems. In the merman poems the setting is the sea. Not only does the sea have metaphoric meaning, but it is an organic part of the poems, whose force is communicated through the sea–land dialectic and the alienation of the merman who wanders forlornly in both spheres. In the Marguerite poems, however, the setting is Switzerland. The richly symbolic sea has been reduced to a rhetorical device—an explanatory metaphor. Even in "To Marguerite—Continued," which is a partial exception, we learn immediately that the sea is not a real, but an allegorical "sea of life."

In "A Summer Night" the change in the meaning of Arnold's sea symbolism is quite plain. The poem opens in a "deserted, moon-blanch'd street," which reminds the speaker of a "past night" when

> Headlands stood out into the moonlit deep
> As clearly as at noon;
> The spring-tide's brimming flow
> Heaved dazzlingly between.

This description, so reminiscent of the close of "The Forsaken Merman," gives rise to a conflict similar to that in the earlier poem, but shaded into quite a different meaning. The land–sea dichotomy is again effective. Most men, we are told, live in a "brazen prison" where they give their lives to "some unmeaning taskwork." A few, however,

> Escape their prison and depart
> On the wide ocean of life anew.
> There the freed prisoner, where'er his heart
> Listeth, will sail.

Storms inevitably strike, reducing the ship to a wreck, with its "pale master"

> Still bent to make some port he knows not where,
> Still standing for some false, impossible shore.

Finally, we lose sight of this unhappy mariner in the gloom, and Arnold asks the agonized question:

> Is there no life, but these alone?
> Madman or slave, must man be one?

The poem ends with an address directed to the heavens, "free from dust and soil," and a final exhortation as ironic as Empedocles' stoic advice to Pausanias at the conclusion of his lecture:

> But I will rather say that you remain
> A world above man's head, to let him see
> How boundless might his soul's horizons be,
> How vast, yet of what clear transparency!
> How it were good to abide there, and breathe free;
> How fair a lot to fill
> Is left to each man still!

The creative life of the sea depths is now seen as a trackless, dangerous setting for a madman. The sea is not a symbol for an imaginative inner realm, but it is an allegorical "ocean of life" with little meaning beyond its function as backdrop for subjective pain and insanity. In the face of this horrifying vision, Arnold once more counsels a stoic passivity somewhere above the real world, abiding in the transparent heavens.

Yet, in another poem by Arnold—"Dover Beach"—the sea is a more organic part of the work and shows a closer symbolic relationship to the merman poetry. "Dover Beach" has been interpreted in many ways and is often associated with Arnold's friendship with Clough.[27] Undoubtedly the poem was influenced by Clough as well as by other sources—Thucydides, Sophocles, and possibly Sainte-Beuve.[28] I feel, nevertheless, that the poem should also be read in the light of Arnold's decision of 1848–1851, especially when that decision has been illuminated by the merman myth.

Although Arnold did not publish "Dover Beach" until 1867, it was probably written earlier, as Tinker and Lowry have pointed out.[29] A draft of the first twenty-eight lines of the poem was penciled on the back of a sheet of paper containing notes on the career of Empedocles. This draft concludes with the words, "Ah love, etc.," which may indicate that the last nine lines of the poem already existed when the portion concerning the sea at Dover was composed.[30] Possibly, Arnold began the last nine lines of the poem as a Marguerite lyric, to which he later added the sea imagery characteristic of his merman poems. "Dover Beach" provides a moving, though melancholy, continuation of Arnold's mythic formulation of the personal decision we have been examining. Such an interpretation would solve the critical problem of a sea poem that ends with an image of a night battle on a plain.[31] The sea–land dichotomy of the merman poems

27. See P. Turner, "Dover Beach and *The Bothie of Tobernavuolich,*" *ES,* 28 (1947), 173–98; B. Trawick, "The Sea of Faith and the Battle by Night in 'Dover Beach,' " *PMLA,* 65 (1950), 1282–83; D.A. Robertson, " 'Dover Beach' and 'say not the struggle naught availeth,' " *PMLA,* 66 (1951), 919–20; P.F. Baum, "Clough and Matthew Arnold," *MLN,* 67 (1952), 546–47.

28. See *Commentary,* 175 ff.; and C.C. Clark, "A Possible Source of Matthew Arnold's 'Dover Beach,' " *MLN,* 17 (1902), 484–85.

29. See "Arnold's 'Dover Beach,' " *TLS* (October 10, 1935), 631; and *Commentary,* 173–75.

30. *Commentary,* 174, 175.

31. See, for instance, F.A. Pottle, *Expl.,* 2 (1944), 45, for an adverse criticism of what Pottle calls "a decided shift in the point of view" between the beginning and end of the poem.

would thereby be extended to "Dover Beach" and we could see, joined in one poem, the abstract metaphors of the Switzerland poems and the suggestive sea symbolism of "The Forsaken Merman." The dominant voice in the poem is not that of an Empedocles, reasoning unhappily on the imprisoning determinism of circumstance and the failure of art. It is instead the plaintive voice of the merman singing sadly by the sea.

"Dover Beach," with its calm sea, its "sweet" night air, its "moon-blanch'd land," its cliffs, and "eternal note of sadness," reminds us of "A Summer Night" and especially of the end of "The Forsaken Merman" and the merman's imagining a last search for the lost Margaret

> at midnight,
> When soft the winds blow,
> When clear falls the moonlight,
> When spring-tides are low;
> When sweet airs come seaward
> From heaths starr'd with broom,
> And high rocks throw mildly
> On the blanch'd sands a gloom.

The ebb tide of the Sea of Faith in "Dover Beach," which retreats down the bare beaches of the world, is anticipated by the merman's hopeless search

> Up the still, glistening beaches,
> Up the creeks we will hie,
> Over banks of bright seaweed
> The ebb-tide leaves dry.

In "Dover Beach" the metamorphosis of the merman is complete. The decision has been made, and the merman has come up from the ocean to live on the land. Yet, despite God's approval of the choice (as in the revised "Neckan"), the consequences of his decision become cruelly plain—as they were in the last stanza of that poem. Once the sea has been abandoned, there can be no return. The sea of faith and love that had once been the

Imagery

merman's home retreats from him, leaving him, as in "The Neckan," an alien in a world whose hidden horror now becomes apparent in the striking image of the night battle on the plain. _— Alienation_

An interesting light illumines this theme of the retreat of the sea in Arnold's letter to Clough of September 29, 1848, the first letter in which he hinted of the existence of Marguerite. In mentioning some dirty water he has seen in Switzerland, Arnold speaks of "the real pain it occasions to one who looks upon water as the Mediator between the inanimate and man."[32] It is possible that this strange remark of Arnold is more significant than it seems at first reading. Could it be that Arnold has pictured in "Dover Beach" the removal of this sacred intermediary to represent symbolically the "high and dry" chaos of human life away from the depths, the final confrontation of man with the brutal insensitivity of a mechanical universe? In the merman poems and in "The Buried Life," water is an intermediary in the sense that it is associated with the creative imagination. The sea depths represent the poetic and mythic vision that can create a reality usable by the human spirit. Its withdrawal, associated with the loss of Marguerite, leaves no channel of communication "between the inanimate and man." In this reading, Arnold, the metamorphosed merman, can only cling pathetically to his Margaret of the land, looking with melancholy foreboding toward his future life as a land-dweller.

> Ah, love, let us be true
> To one another! for the world, which seems
> To lie before us like a land of dreams,
> So various, so beautiful, so new,
> Hath really neither joy, nor love, nor light,
> Nor certitude, nor peace, nor help for pain;
> And we are here as on a darkling plain

32. _Letters to Clough_, 92.

Swept with confused alarms of struggle and flight,
Where ignorant armies clash by night.

Although Arnold's poetry does occasionally move to a third stage of calm and to active service in the world, its emotional and artistic center is found in "Dover Beach," where the youth of "The Strayed Reveller," now mature, paces in thought. He has achieved the beauty of the gods' vision, but not without the suffering of the bards. We cannot think of Matthew Arnold's poetry without the haunting, lovely, and hopeless cry sounding in our ears: "And we are *here* as on a darkling plain."

*   *   *   *

Nevertheless, we may view "Tristram and Iseult," the last and most ambitious of the poems related to Marguerite and the sea, as a powerful attempt to move into a third stage of calm or of active service, to escape the darkling plain. In a sense, the third part of the poem, "Iseult of Brittany," concluding as it does with a summarizing myth, implies that art may be, after all, a useful tool for the troubled human spirit. Yet, the content of the final Merlin emblem and its context within the larger poem modify Arnold's view of art here into something far different.

If it is true, as I contend, that Arnold's progressive loss of faith in poetry as a creative mode of knowledge is associated with his loss of Marguerite, a human image of his art, then "Tristram and Iseult" is the culminating event in the process. The poem has been associated, for instance, with "The Church of Brou," whose heroine is the Duchess Marguerite. We know also that "Tristram and Iseult" was first conceived at Thun, where he encountered the story in a French review. Apparently the poem was conceived when there was only one Iseult in Arnold's life and completed when there were two.[33]

33. *Commentary*, 109; Culler, 121 and 140.

With such obvious biographical relationships, it is tempting to make allegorical identifications of the three characters in Arnold's poem to the three participants in his own life drama: Iseult of Ireland to Marguerite, Iseult of Brittany to Frances Wightman, and Tristram to Arnold himself. Such easy identifications are to be resisted. "No Arnold could ever write a novel," Arnold is supposed to have said, and this dictum applies to his poetry.[34] The characters in his poems are not developed as individual human beings so much as they are created to symbolize states of mind and life styles. The conflict in "Tristram and Iseult" follows this pattern. There is no struggle between the two Iseults; they do not even meet. Although the story is based on sexual passion, there is little direct presentation of it in the poem: that is, Tristram and the two Iseults are not sharply defined in terms of male and female. Instead, Tristram and Iseult of Ireland compose a passionate pair over against the gentle Iseult of Brittany. What we have here is closely similar to what we have in "Empedocles on Etna": three modes of life brought into a tense and painful juxtaposition that results in catastrophe. In "Tristram and Iseult" the three characters do more than present themselves dramatically as do the three in "Empedocles." They are also brought together and judged by Arnold's pseudomedieval narrator, who is "not Arnold," but who is surely Arnold's means of imaginatively testing the three points of view as was Empedocles.

In the figure of Tristram are many of the mythic and symbolic terms Arnold has used previously. He is associated with the innocent "forest glade"; he is an unhappy lover; he is a poet who is known by his "harp of gold"; and he is an alien in exile. His name is "Sorrow." If we substitute sea caverns for forest glade, Tristram is very like the forsaken merman. The narrator portrays him in "his exiled loneliness," and on

34. A. Dwight Culler, "No Arnold Could Ever Write a Novel," *VNL* (Spring 1966), 1.

> His long rambles by the shore
> On winter-evenings, when the roar
> Of the near waves came, sadly grand,
> Through the dark, up the drown'd sand.

Like the Neckan, Tristram tries to solve his problems by entering society, by taking action in the wars of King Arthur. But neither solitude nor action helps. "The rushing battle cleared thy blood / As little as did solitude." He is haunted—significantly, when we remember "Dover Beach" and Arnold's feeling about water—by the image of Iseult appearing in a spring:

> Mild shines the cold spring in the moon's clear light;
> God! 'tis *her* face plays in the waters bright.

In the terms of "A Summer Night" Tristram is the "madman" who is cast adrift on a stormy ocean of subjective passion. His manic wanderings, recalled in feverish dreams, result in irresponsibility, faithlessness, and finally death.

Iseult of Ireland is the least developed of the three characters of the poem. Her description tallies with the conventional description of the "passionate" heroines of the Victorian novel, Eustacia Vye, Bathsheba Everdene, even Maggie Tulliver. She has "proud dark eyes," "raven hair," "the old imperious air," and she gives "petulant replies." Although Arnold suggests his characteristic dichotomy between subjective alienation and external action by having Iseult describe Tristram as a "pining exile in thy forest" and herself as "a smiling queen upon my throne," it is clear, from the context of her conversation with Tristram, that both of them symbolize the same state of madness, induced by "some tyrannous single thought, some fit / Of passion, which subdues our souls to it." In Tristram's tryst with her on the "pleasaunce-walks," he calls her "Madcap." The similarity between Tristram and the Irish Iseult becomes more apparent in Arnold's treatment of Part II, "Iseult of Ireland." It is only 193 lines long (compared to 373 for "Tristram" and

224 for "Iseult of Brittany") and is devoted, not to a description of her, but to a final conversation between her and Tristram—approximately half the section—up to the lovers' unexplained death. The last 93 lines are devoted to the narrator's description of the scene and the introduction of the Huntsman in the tapestry.

The lyrical description of the lifeless lovers by the narrator and the symbolism of the stately Huntsman have aroused the interest of all the critics of the poem and caused no little mystification. I think that, in order to understand this passage, we must see the first two parts of the poem as being essentially one, as expressing through both characters the problem of "A Summer Night": Is there no other possibility in life but to be mad, as Tristram and Iseult both are in their lawless passion, or slaves, as Tristram is in his service to Arthur and conventional married life, or as Iseult is, playing her courtly role as Marc's queen, her "aching brow . . . circled . . . by a band of gold"?

This human problem has an aesthetic parallel (as in "The Strayed Reveller" or the merman poetry): May poetry exist as a valid experience without being overwhelmed by the unstable vagaries of subjective passion? Arnold's answer to these questions at the end of Part II of "Tristram and Iseult" is a highly qualified yes. In the beautiful lines of the conclusion to the section, the tumult of the lovers' active lives has been transfigured to a symbol of lasting beauty. The time-bound and hopeless struggles of Tristram and Iseult have been fixed, as it were, and elevated to an eternal and transcendent realm out of time.

Arnold has drawn here upon the tradition of Keats, especially as expressed in "The Eve of St. Agnes" or the "Grecian Urn." Harmony and the serene Apollonian vision lend permanent aesthetic significance to human affairs. It is important for us to see how Arnold achieves these qualities. The chief means for this luminous epiphany in "Tristram and Iseult," as in "Empedocles on Etna" or even in "Sohrab and Rustum," is death. Tristram and Iseult are beautiful when they are motionless and frozen in a passive tableau:

> Cold, cold as those who lived and loved
> A thousand years ago.

The message of the poem up to this point has been that in life the lovers were helpless against the imprisoning circumstances of a hostile world and the instability of their own restless hearts. Action of any sort has been hopeless; the only escape from their unhappiness has been a passive resignation to the unconsciousness of death. Tristram's death is caused by a wound; Iseult's is —physiologically speaking—quite unaccountable. Death, the narrator tells us, erases the "ravages of time" from Iseult's appearance and restores

> A tranquil, settled loveliness,
> Her younger rival's purest grace.

The relationship of the death of the lovers to art is established by the introduction of the Huntsman on the arras, which moves in the cold December air like the tapestry of "The Eve of St. Agnes." The Huntsman, in his "fresh forest-scene" recalls the early innocence of Tristram and the innocent first stage of Arnold's poetry, the "forest-glade." He also brings to mind the innocence of the strayed reveller, or the more cruel innocence of the gods as "He gazes down into the room." Although his face is "troubled," perhaps like the wondering concern of the reveller or even the puzzled curiosity of Tennyson's Lancelot gazing at the dead Lady of Shalott, he sees as the gods and reveller do, "without pain, without labour." Like the view from above of the gods, his vision, serene and beautiful as it is, is illusory. His superficial explanation of the presence of Tristram and Iseult is lovely, but false.

> *"What place is this, and who are they?*
> *Who is that kneeling Lady fair?*

And on his pillows that pale Knight
Who seems of marble on a tomb?

. . . .

That Knight's asleep, and at her prayer
That Lady by the bed doth kneel—
Then hush, thou boisterous bugle-peal!"

The fundamental break between the Huntsman's Apollonian vision of the silent, aesthetically pleasing figures of
Tristram and Iseult and the "real" truth about them, the
chasm between life and art, is enunciated by the narrator
as he addresses the Huntsman on the tapestry.

Cheer, cheer thy dogs into the brake,
O Hunter! and without a fear
Thy golden-tassell'd bugle blow,
And through the glades thy pastime take—
For thou wilt rouse no sleepers here!
For these thou seest are unmoved;
Cold, cold as those who lived and loved
A thousand years ago.

Arnold has given us a myth, then, of piercing beauty,
which reveals his growing feeling that art and myth, while
very possibly therapeutic, are illusory. The narrator is not
part of the myth; he interprets it. He is the rational man
telling the truth that art has, for the moment, obscured.
Arnold has sympathized with Keats's presentation of the
problem in "The Eve of St. Agnes" and the "Grecian
Urn," but has been unable to progress to the even more
profound Keatsian insights of "Ode to a Nightingale" or
"Autumn." The troubled face of the Huntsman reflects
not only his inability to grasp the significance of the
deathbed scene, but also Arnold's distress at the inability
of the poetic imagination to deal with life itself.

Everything that we have seen so far of Arnold's
poetry leads us to expect what we do in fact find in Part
III. Here Iseult of Brittany is "settling for" what all of
Arnold's protagonists come to settle for—stoic passivity.
We must not commit here the most common of critical

71

crimes: the assertion that everything is like everything else. "Iseult of Brittany" is not to be assimilated to what I have called the "gratuitous" conclusions of "The Strayed Reveller," "A Summer Night," Empedocles' lecture, or even "The Neckan." Although this ending is similar in intent, it is more imaginative and more fully realized. Arnold has reached his decision through his private process. The volume in which this poem first appeared was withdrawn the following year. Paradoxically, "Iseult of Brittany" is Arnold's most complete and most imaginative statement of his loss of faith in the creative imagination.

There are two central symbols by which Arnold conveys his message: one is the life situation in which Iseult and her children exist; the other is the emblematic myth of Merlin and Vivian, which concludes the poem. Arnold's symbolic method is similar to the first two parts, in which the situation of Tristram and Iseult is contrasted to the emblem of the Huntsman.

The scene of Part III is one of cold beauty. Iseult has taken her children to a protected "green circular hollow" by the seashore to play. The isolated spot and the activities of the widowed mother and children are nonsexual, strictly regulated. The colors are muted. But the scene is not equivalent to the walled village of "The Forsaken Merman." The stark winter scene is suited to represent imaginatively the stoic advice given in so many of Arnold's earlier poems.

> The heather, which all round
> Creeps thickly, grows not here; but the pale grass
> Is strewn with rocks, and many a shiver'd mass
> Of vein'd white-gleaming quartz, and here and there
> Dotted with holly-trees and juniper.
> In the smooth centre of the opening stood
> Three hollies side by side, and made a screen,
> Warm with the winter-sun, of burnish'd green
> With scarlet berries gemm'd, the fell-fare's food.
> Under the glittering hollies Iseult stands,

Watching her children play; their little hands
Are busy gathering spars of quartz, and streams
Of stagshorn for their hats.

This is not the generative, creative environment of the
sea caverns nor does it touch on a "buried life." Instead,
it is a beautiful representation of how to make the best
of the "given": a winter sun, white rocks, green holly, and
red berries. This scene of the children playing in the
midst of nonillusory reality contrasts vividly with the enchanted landscape outside the children's window when
the "tired madcaps" are imagined asleep in Part I.

To see the park-glades where you play
Far lovelier than they are by day,
To see the sparkle on the eaves,
And upon every giant-bough
Of those old oaks, whose wet red leaves
Are jewell'd with bright drops of rain.

Or they might see beyond the castle park

The bare heaths spreading, clear as day,
Moor behind moor, far, far away,
Into the heart of Brittany.
And here and there, lock'd by the land,
Long inlets of smooth glittering sea,
And many a stretch of watery sand
All shining in the white moon-beams.

In Part I, the sleeping children are surrounded by a shim-
mering moonlit fairyland where raindrops appear to be
jewels, and the land, interspersed by "glittering sea,"
stretches out to the center of the Celtic imagination,
"Into the heart of Brittany." In Part III, they are wide
awake under a winter sun, gathering stones on the dormant heath.

When the children's cheeks become flushed and
their hair unruly from active play on the heath, Iseult calls
them to her to tell them "an old-world Breton history,"
the story of Merlin and Vivian. We learn, significantly,

that their looks did not "stray once to the sea-side." But before Arnold allows the story itself to be told, he introduces two more elements into the treatment of Iseult's situation: the narrator's description of Iseult's daily life and the much-discussed moralizing section (ll. 112–150), which Arnold removed briefly from the poem, but reinserted in 1857. The narrator first asks if Iseult is "happy." The answer is that she is not. "Joy," the life-giving spirit so necessary for romantics like Wordsworth is impossible.

> Joy has not found her yet, nor ever will—
>
> . . . .
>
> She moves slow; her voice alone
> Hath yet an infantine and silver tone,
> But even that comes languidly; in truth,
> She seems one dying in a mask of youth.

This description of Iseult is extremely suggestive. The picture of the young mother with her "infantine" voice, another child among her children, leads one to sympathize with Norman Holland's provocative view that Victorians, and especially Arnold, "sought parents such as a child could wish, parents devoid of sexuality."[35] I am not concerned to prove Holland's Freudian interpretation of Arnold's poetry and Victorian society, but his researches, although proceeding from different assumptions, are analogous to my own. The final part of "Tristram and Iseult" is characterized by childlike passivity. The generative possibilities of the first two parts are lost.

> Yes, it is lonely for her in her hall.
> The children, and the grey-hair'd seneschal,
> Her women, and Sir Tristram's aged hound,
> Are there the sole companions to be found.

Iseult's only social stimulation is her children, and she is with them "night and day." Her pursuits are very like the pursuits of Margaret in "The Forsaken Merman"—

35. "Psychological Depths and 'Dover Beach,'" *VS*, Supplement to Vol. 9 (September 1965), 22.

monotonous activity and monotonous prayer, isolated from the creative energies of life. At bedtime she will rise

> And at her prie-dieu kneel, until she have told
> Her rosary-beads of ebony tipp'd with gold,
> Then to her soft sleep—and to-morrow'll be
> To-day's exact repeated effigy.

In the first part of the poem we saw her—like the merman—"Watching by the salt sea-tide / With her children at her side." The childlike Iseult is incapable of imaginative creation in her life and can only copy what is "given" in "exactly repeated" effigies. In "The For-saken Merman," the choice between modes of life was kept open. The merman and Margaret symbolized two active, live options for the young Arnold. In "Tristram and Iseult" the two options have, in a sense, been imaginatively fused, although many of the qualities of the merman have vanished. Tristram and Iseult of Ireland are dead, and all of Arnold's imaginative capital has been converted into the dramatic and mythic portrayal of the possibilities of life without the presence of dynamic creativity. Iseult of Brittany is not only analogous to the forsaken merman or to Margaret, but she is also a much fuller representation of the Neckan, in whose situation art is not vision, but is a "help for pain" or, as Holland would say in his Freudian terminology, a "defence."[36] The Breton tales Iseult loves, beautiful as they are, are used to "beguile" the children benignly and to cause Iseult her-self to "forget all to hear them."

I must agree with the many critics who feel that Arnold erred in aesthetic judgment by allowing the nar-rator's didactic commentary (ll. 112–150) to remain in the poem. The delicate interplay of the characters and the external point of view of the medieval storyteller, so skillfully handled in the treatment of the Huntsman, here breaks down. When we understand the intention of the poem as a whole, Arnold's need to interject this direct

36. "Psychological Depths," 10.

commentary becomes clearer. It is not just that he wants to reiterate the opposition of the "gradual furnace of the world" to the "tyrannous single thought" (slave vs. madman) more directly and to reject both—especially the "fool passion," which has such important biographical significance; a more important consideration shaped his presentation of Iseult of Brittany. Despite the beauty of his portrayal of the lonely Iseult, I think Arnold was aware of some of the weaknesses this imaginative and honest portrayal suggested. He felt a strong need to portray her joyless life and, perhaps more important, to justify his new attitude to art. He must insist that it is passion and worldliness that prevent art, not passive suffering. He must assert once more that art is valuable, not for its creative vision, but for its ability to move us therapeutically.

> Dear saints, it is not sorrow, as I hear,
> Not suffering, which shuts up eye and ear
> To all that has delighted them before,
> And lets us be what we were once no more.
> No, we may suffer deeply, yet retain
> Power to be moved and soothed, for all our pain,
> By what of old pleased us, and will again.

The use of passive voice is significant and pathetic. The romantic urge for power to make and to see is now a "Power to be moved and soothed." The necessity to feel, even when one has the power, is far different from the necessity to see and create.

The meaning of the myth of Merlin and Vivian is extremely complex. This concluding emblem for the entire poem has several meanings, some of which belie the apparent intention of the poem as a whole. In attempting to assess its significance, it is necessary to view it in its several possible contexts. First of all, we must remember that the story is told by Iseult to her children; then we must recall that the medieval narrator is also telling the story for his purposes; finally, we must be aware that Arnold created all. In such a series of Chinese boxes, we must not be surprised if we find more than one prize.

Reflecting on the Merlin and Vivian story from the point of view of the narrator, who has just delivered his lecture on this "fool passion," we come to something like the traditional interpretation of its significance. Merlin is to be equated roughly to Tristram, and Vivian to Iseult of Ireland, despite Vivian's faithlessness. The story becomes a nearly perfect medieval exemplum, illustrating the narrator's sermon specifically and the whole poem by analogy. The downfall of Merlin represents the sin of lust and the untrustworthiness of women. The wisdom of the past teaches that life is a serious business; it is to be led neither in worldliness nor in frivolous passion. One can easily imagine either Chaucer's clerk or the Wife of Bath's fourth husband telling the tale.

When we consider the story from Iseult's point of view, we see that she is using it, as the narrator says, to "beguile" the children in the midst of their restless activity. In another sense it is a transfiguration of her own experience, as the Huntsman is a transfiguration of the death of Tristram. In fantasy, she recounts the tale of a man who succumbs to the power of another woman, and is entrapped by her. In this fantasy portrayal, her rival tires of the love affair and leaves her lover asleep in the woods. Not only does the fantasy work the downfall of two people who have given her pain, but further possibilities emerge as we enter more deeply into the thorny mazes of Broce-liande. If Merlin is indeed analogous to Tristram and his entrapment analogous to Tristram's obsession with "some tyrannous single thought," the description can only be regarded as inept. Merlin is never described as being overcome by passion. He does not risk his life for a tryst with Vivian or engage himself in knight errantry to forget her. Instead, he

> Forgot his craft, and his best wits took flight;
> And he grew fond, and eager to obey
> His mistress, use her empire as she may.

Even the dying Tristram could never be thought of as "fond, and eager to obey." Merlin and Vivian come to a halt when they find a resting place. Merlin has, in this treatment of the story, no impulses in the vernal wood, sexual, emotional, or intellectual.

> They sate them down together, and a sleep
> Fell upon Merlin, more like death, so deep.

There is simply a passive acceptance of his fate. Sleep and a deathlike unconsciousness replace the powers of Merlin, the magician and, more significantly, the seer. In a sense then, Iseult has cast Merlin in her own image. It is possible, in a weird paradox, to see Merlin as analogous to Iseult and Vivian as analogous to the faithless Tristram; we need not think this role reversal unlikely, after the examples of Arnold's propensity for the device in the merman poems or the Marguerite poems. When we examine the telling of the story in context—the three figures in the sheltered, wintry hollow, the serious young eyes riveted to the child mother—we may wonder if, as J. L. Kendall says, Iseult and her children are not moving into the same dormant entrapment as Merlin's.[37]

Finally, we must look at Merlin from Arnold's point of view, set in the context not only of "Tristram and Iseult" but of all the poems that led up to it. For Arnold, the issues involved in the work were both aesthetic and personal. In his rational conception of the poem, I believe he shared some of the sentiments of his narrator. His poem is a dramatic presentation of two lives destroyed and one life impoverished as a result of passion. Thus the story of Merlin's destruction by the fickle Vivian seemed an appropriate way to fix and make significant the action. But we must not forget that Arnold was also at the culmination of a process of decision about his life and work. He was approaching a conclusion about the function of poetry, for which his most vivid personal symbol was his relation to Marguerite. Arnold may consciously have thought of himself as being related to both Tristram and

37. "The Unity of Arnold's 'Tristram and Iseult,'" *VP*, 1 (April 1963), 145.

Merlin because they were passionate lovers whose love brought about catastrophe. Vivian's blue eyes, her "mocking glee," and her "fresh clear grace" cannot fail to remind us of Marguerite. "When we read in the last few lines of the poem," Culler writes, "that Merlin was immured by Vivian in a 'daisied circle' and recall that the French word for daisy is *marguerite*, it is almost as if Arnold had left his personal signature in one corner of his painting."[38] But there is a more unconscious signature indelibly marked on Arnold's treatment of the story. Arnold is not really like Merlin and Tristram because he is a passionate lover; he gave up Marguerite and returned home to marry Frances Wightman. He is like Merlin and Tristram because he is a poet. And with his loss of belief in his creative powers, he is, like Merlin, asleep, imprisoned in an enchanted forest. As figured in the merman poems and the Marguerite poems, he has not decided to relinquish his powers; they have been nullified by an external agency, in this case Vivian–Marguerite, in whom he has placed all his trust and who has shown herself faithless and "passing weary of his love." The sleeping Merlin, powerless to see or feel the world about him, is the perfect symbol to sum up the result of Arnold's decision and his subsequent vision of himself: a poet who has no belief in the creative power of poetry.

It is my contention that Arnold wrote far better than he knew. It is an ironic truth that "Tristram and Iseult," perhaps Arnold's loveliest and most imaginative poem, records with poignant clarity his loss of faith in the poetic imagination. Yet, if it is true that what we know are symbols; if it is true that myth provides the reality from which various truths may be derived, then "Tristram and Iseult" is a proof-text. It is not the rational lecture of his narrator but Arnold's creative and imaginative vision that makes us "see," that makes us "know," that, contrary to Arnold's own voice in the 1853 Preface, makes us "rejoice."

38. Culler, 151. See also Honan, "Arnold in Love."

Although we can observe the shaping of Arnold's decision about poetry and Marguerite as it is formulated in his best poems, there is an epilogue to the story. It is no part of my present concern to trace the consequences of Arnold's later attitude to imaginative literature in his critical career, as tempting as it is to do so. But there are a few questions that must be answered. If, for instance, "Empedocles" represents, like "Tristram and Iseult," Arnold's loss of faith in the cognitive power of poetry, why did he withdraw the earlier poem and write the famous Preface of 1853 to explain his reasons? If the decision we have been discussing resulted in Arnold's virtual abandonment of his poetic career, why did he take the trouble to outline a new poetics in that Preface and to illustrate it with what is undoubtedly his most ambitious work, "Sohrab and Rustum"?[39]

The answers to these questions seem relatively clear, once we understand the meaning of what has gone before. D. G. James, in his excellent treatment of Arnold's criticism, *Matthew Arnold and the Decline of English Romanticism,* has put his finger precisely on the source of the trouble. Arnold, in James's view, was dissatisfied with the basic principle of the romantic movement, the autonomy of poetry, and was therefore searching—somewhat desperately—for a doctrine that would validate the importance of poetry.[40] His later criticism is full of appeals to "emotion," to "culture," or to the "idea." If poetry is not a valid mode of knowing in itself, is there something else that can make it so?

Arnold first attempted to establish the "something else" in the Preface to the 1853 edition of *Poems* by invoking Aristotle's principles and Greek dramatic litera-

39. Culler writes (195) that, "had *The Scholar Gipsy* been finished in time to be published in the volume of 1852 along with *Empedocles on Etna,* it would have been rejected along with that poem in the Preface of 1853."
40. (Oxford, Oxford University Press, 1961), 81.

ture as sane, objective, and permanent measuring sticks by which to evaluate the fragmented subjectivism of "modern literature," "the dialogue of the mind with it- self," or, as Arnold described it in a quotation from a contemporaneous critic, "a true allegory of the state of one's own mind in a representative history." The bases for our love of poetry, Arnold says, are two: accurate representation and poetry's ability to "inspirit and rejoice the reader"; that is, poetry must imitate life and it must be therapeutic: "For the Muses, as Hesiod says, were born that they might be 'a forgetfulness of evils, and a truce from cares.'" Arnold then asks what kind of situa- tions fail to nurture this necessary therapeutic quality in poetry:

> They are those in which the suffering finds no vent in action; in which a continuous state of mental distress is prolonged, unrelieved by incident, hope, or resistance; in which there is everything to be endured, nothing to be done. In such situations there is inevitably something mor- bid, in the description of them something monotonous. When they occur in actual life, they are painful, not tragic; the representation of them in poetry is painful also.

Arnold then places Empedocles in this class of situations. It is from our vantage point easy to see that all of Arnold's best poems to some extent fall into this class of situations, including his two most important poems in the new vol- ume, "Sohrab and Rustum" and "The Scholar-Gipsy."

It is important for us to understand what Arnold has said here and what he has not said. He has not denied that "Empedocles" is a true allegory of the state of his own mind. Indeed, this is exactly why he has withdrawn it and why he is so dissatisfied with all his "fragmented" earlier poetry. Yet Arnold's use of Aristotle is somewhat slippery. Aeschylus' *Prometheus* and Sophocles' *Oedipus*, for in- stance, really have no more "vent in action" than Em- pedocles, whose suicide is presented as a positive act. Arnold insists also, however, that the *situation* of the Empedocles story is not suitable for poetic expression. One of Aristotle's chief criteria for good drama was its ability to produce catharsis among the audience. With this criterion in mind, why should the suicide of Empedocles as a situation be less cathartic for a Victorian reader than Oedipus' destruction of his eyes for an Athenian playgoer? Arnold is being far more subjective in this manifesto of classicism than he pretends. The fact is that the symbol of a poet who cannot believe in poetry is too painful for its author. It is Arnold himself who sees "no vent in action," who has found himself in a "continuous state of mental distress . . . in which there is everything to be endured, nothing to be done." The trouble with "Empedocles" is not so much that the work is itself "unrelieved by incident, hope, or resistance" or that it has not been able to "inspirit and rejoice the reader," but that it has not been able to "inspirit and rejoice" Arnold.

What follows is what we might expect. Since Arnold doubts the cognitive possibilities of poetry and the creative function of the human mind, he must find an objective basis upon which to erect poetry, a basis inherently superior to the subjective and devoid of its problems. This basis, Arnold tells us, is great actions, and for instructive poetic models we must go to the ancients' treatment of them. The rest of Arnold's essay exemplifies the fragmentation of words, things, and reality. Ironically, it is an exercise in the separation of form and content, although it purports to be a plea for a unified art. Thus, Arnold says in contrasting modern poets with the Greeks that "with us, attention is fixed mainly on the value of the separate thoughts and images which occur in the treatment of an action. They regarded the whole; we regard the parts. With them, the action predominates over the expression of it; with us, expression predominates over the action." Again, Arnold terms Greek "expression" excellent "because it draws its force directly from the pregnancy of the matter which it conveys." Here we see something at least related to positivist assumptions. By "the whole" Arnold implies "the matter," the objective facts that are "real" and for which poetic expression is to be an ornament. The "matter" he regards as antecedent to its poetic or mythic formulation and as being in no important sense dependent upon its shaping. The model of Greek literature, to follow Arnold's thinking, proclaims: "All depends upon the subject; choose a fitting action, penetrate yourself with the feeling of its situations; this done, everything else will follow." Arnold then laments the "critics who seem to direct their attention merely to detached expressions, to the language about the action, not to the action itself." Those who have commerce with the ancients "are more truly than others under the empire of facts, and more independent of the language current among those with whom they live."

Allen Tate wrote of Arnold's poetic theory: "On the one side it is an eighteenth-century view of poetic language as the rhetorical vehicle of ideas; and it is connected with Arnold's famous definition of religion as 'morality touched with emotion.' Poetry is descriptive science or experience at that level, touched with emotion."[41] Not only is this the eighteenth-century mirror aesthetic we have encountered earlier; it is also a mature and more honest version of the aesthetic of the youthful reveller who saw "Without pain, without labour."

But what are we to say about "Sohrab and Rustum," the prime illustration of Arnold's new poetics? The first comment, I think, is that while it is a fine poem and while it attempts to adhere—almost pedantically—to the external stylistic habits of Homer, it is in fact no more an illustration of the doctrines of the Preface of 1853 than "Tristram and Iseult." In fact the massive, if anachronistic, attempt to reproduce an epic style works in direct opposition to the warnings of the Preface against too much attention to "expression," which fixes our attention "mainly on the value of the separate thoughts and images which occur in the treatment of an action." The action of the poem itself treats a movement from ignorance, caused in the main by passion and pride, to a sad enlightenment, to Sohrab's death and Rustum's grief, which is

41. *Collected Essays*, 18.

mitigated only by his stoic endurance. The violent action of father and son is contrasted to Sohrab's promise of final peace for his father and the famous concluding symbol of the majestic river as it floats

> Rejoicing, through the hush'd Chorasmian waste,
> Under the solitary moon;—he flow'd
> Right for the polar star, past Orgunjè;
> Brimming, and bright, and large; then sands begin
> To hem his watery march, and dam his streams,
> And split his currents; that for many a league
> The shorn and parcell'd Oxus strains along
> Through beds of sand and matted rushy isles—
> Oxus, forgetting the bright speed he had
> In his high mountain-cradle in Pamere,
> A foil'd circuitous wanderer—till at last
> The long'd-for dash of waves is heard, and wide
> His luminous home of waters opens, bright
> And tranquil, from whose floor the new-bathed stars
> Emerge, and shine upon the Aral Sea.

In this lyrical and un-Homeric image, Arnold returned to the moon-lit ocean that figured so emphatically in his earlier poems of struggle. It is no longer the sea of faith, but is the wide-glimmering sea of Culler's three-stage formulation. It is reached, not by action or imaginative effort, but by floating through the divisive sands and islands on its course until it is received by the ocean. The eternal heavens and the madman's ocean of "A Summer Night" are fused in this lovely symbol of stoic passivity and peace.

One critic has suggested that "Rustum, as the grizzled man of war—stern, bitter, aloof—is a military version of Empedocles, and that Sohrab, the fresh, glancing youth, is closely akin to Callicles."[42] I should like to suggest further that, despite his disclaimers in the Preface, Arnold had once more produced an allegory of the state of his own mind in a representative history. I think

42. Culler, 208.

that in the consenting death of Sohrab and in the endur-
ing survival of Rustum on the darkling plain, we have a
symbol of the process Arnold had undergone in coming
to peace with himself. The son lives on, not in the father,
but in the majestic monument the father raises to com-
memorate the death of his son—in Arnold's case, the
poem. It was Arnold's own pleasure in composing the
poem and finally settling his future that caused him to
admire it so much, not its supposed adherence to Aristotle's principles. Arnold wrote a revealing quatrain, which
he used as a prefatory note to "Sohrab and Rustum" and
which he sent to Clough, saying it was "terribly true":[43]

> What Poets feel not, when they make,
> A pleasure in creating,
> The world, in *its* turn, will not take
> Pleasure in contemplating.

It is often said that the Preface of 1853 and "Sohrab
and Rustum" mark Arnold's movement from a subjective
poetry to an objective poetry. Rather, these two works are
a subjective and a creative symbol for his movement from
the role of creative artist to that of critic who sees things
as in themselves they really are and who defends poetry
because it attaches its emotion to ideas rather than facts.
To my mind, the significance of Arnold's career lies in its
pathos. He did not turn away from the modern impasse
between the claims of the creative imagination and the
claims of positivism. He attempted, with a creative mind
of genius and a poetic temperament, to live by positivist
rules in a positivist world but to remain untouched by
them. In his courageous failure may be seen the more
general failure of modern poetry to come to terms with
the problem of knowledge. Dante's Paradise could not
have been created without Beatrice. Arnold's City of God
lost the full power and meaning of its beginnings when
the poet abandoned the role of a merman in love with a
girl for the role of Headmaster of Victorian England.

43. *Letters to Clough*, 126.

III.

GERARD MANLEY HOPKINS: THE STRUGGLE WITH DEISM

I look out on earth . . . lo, all is chaos;
I look at heaven . . . its light is gone;
I look out on the mountains . . . they are trembling;
And all the hills are swaying!
I look out . . . lo, no man is to be seen;
All the birds have flown!
I look out . . . lo, the sown land lies a desert;
And the towns are all razed by the Lord's rage.
For thus has the Lord said:
The whole land shall be desolate . . .
And for this shall the earth mourn
And the heavens above be black.
I have purposed it and will not repent;
Neither will I turn back from it. . . .
Every city shall be abandoned,
And not a man dwell therein.
You ruined creature, what will you do!
      —Jeremiah 4 : 23–30

Or what is else? There is your world within.
There rid the dragons, root out there the sin.
Your will is law in that small commonweal. . . .
      —Gerard Manley Hopkins

LANGUAGE AND THEOLOGY

In his notorious attack on Hopkins, Yvor Winters began where all commentators must—with Hopkins'

Portions of this chapter appeared as "Gerard Manley Hopkins and the 'Stanching, Quenching Ocean of a Motionable Mind' " in *Victorian Newsletter* (Fall 1966). It has been incor-

distinctive use of language, his idiosyncratic attitude toward words. In establishing his criteria for judging Hopkins, Winters declared his own attitude toward words—an attitude directly related to the problems of language, perception, and imaginative creation with which so many nineteenth-century poets wrestled. "Words," Winters wrote, "are primarily conceptual: the words *grief, tree, poetry, God,* represent concepts; they may communicate some feeling and remembered sensory impression as well, and they may be made to communicate a great deal of these, but they will do it by virtue of their conceptual identity, and in so far as this identity is impaired they will communicate less of these and communicate them with less force and precision."[1] The view that words "represent concepts" to be defined, that they stand for a "conceptual identity" separate from the speaker, and for that identity solely, is surely related to the general proposition that reality exists outside the self and must be represented by concepts of remembered qualities. Implicit in Winters' definition is the belief that words (and by extension poems) are tools for communicating concepts or identities that exist autonomously from the articulation of the words or poems.

Hopkins' theory and practice of language is very much opposed to Winters' theory. What has made Hopkins' work so distinctive among the Victorians and so attractive to the contemporary literary mind is precisely his rejection of the often mechanical equivalences of positivism. As early as 1868 Hopkins outlined a fairly sophisticated theory of words and their relation to things, reality, and the self. Although his theory is not fully developed and somewhat tentative, it is worth detailed

---

porated into this essay by permission of the editor, William E. Buckler.

1. "Gerard Manley Hopkins," in *Hopkins: A Collection of Critical Essays,* Geoffrey H. Hartman, ed. (Englewood Cliffs, N.J., Prentice-Hall, Inc., 1966), 37, 38.

examination. "A word then," Hopkins wrote, "has three terms belonging to it, ὅροι or moments—its prepossession of feeling; its definition, abstraction, vocal expression or other utterance; and its application, 'extension,' the concrete things coming under it." The middle term, in Hopkins' theory, is the only one that "in propriety is the word; the third is not a word but a thing meant by it, the first is not a word but something connotatively meant by it, the nature of which is further to be explored." It is in his discussion of the middle term, which seems at first to be analogous to Winters' conceptual definition, that Hopkins' theory characteristically differs from Winters'. "For the word is the expression, *uttering* the idea in the mind. That idea itself has its two terms, the image (of sight or sound or *scapes* of the other senses), which is in fact physical and a refined energy accenting the nerves, a word to oneself, an inchoate word, and *secondly the conception*" (my italics for last phrase).[2] For Hopkins, words are not to be reduced to manipulatable conceptions but are to be allowed a vibrant life of their own, related to the images they evoke, their sound, and their "uttering" in the mind of the speaker, "a word to oneself." Such a view of words will not come as a surprise to anyone familiar with Hopkins' word-play in his diaries and journals. In the same notes Hopkins extended his complex view of words to art.

> Works of art of course like words utter the idea and in representing real things convey the prepossession with more or less success.
> The further in anything, as a work of art, the organization is carried out, the deeper the form penetrates, the prepossession flushes the matter, the more effort will be required in apprehension, the more power of comparison,

2. From *The Journals and Papers of Gerard Manley Hopkins*, Humphry House, ed. (London, published by the Oxford University Press by arrangement with the Society of Jesus, 1959), 125. Hereafter cited as *J*.

> the more capacity for receiving that synthesis of (either successive or spatially distinct) impressions which gives us the unity with the prepossession conveyed by it. (*J*, 126)

Hopkins seems to be suggesting in these somewhat obscure early notes the necessity for a parallel unity of diverse elements both in words themselves and in works of art. In the passage concerned with art, for instance, we learn that the "idea" and the "prepossession" should be conveyed together with careful organization and a continuous effort at appropriate comparisons of diverse parts. "The further . . . the organization is carried out, the deeper the form penetrates, the prepossession flushes the matter." Similarly, "the more power of comparison, the more capacity for receiving that synthesis of . . . impressions which gives us the unity with the prepossession conveyed by it." In these remarks Hopkins not only commented theoretically about language and art, but he made, if unconsciously, an accurate forecast of his own poetic practice and the future reception of his work: when "the prepossession flushes the matter, the more effort will be required in apprehension."

In his conclusion to this group of notes on words, Hopkins described a "saner" and a "less sane" mode of contemplation and expression. Although his notes are brief and cryptic, it is apparent that the saner view, in his mind, was the organic, unified perception, while the less sane was the defining, fragmenting turn of mind we think of as modern.

> The saner moreover is the act of contemplation as contemplating that which really is expressed in the object.
>
> But some minds prefer that the prepossession they are to receive should be conveyed by the least organic, expressive, by the most suggestive, way. By this means the prepossession and the definition, uttering, are distinguished and unwound, which is the less sane attitude. (*J*, 126)

Three years before these notes on language and art, Hopkins had made the same point even more clearly in his essay, "On the Origin of Beauty: A Platonic Dialogue." In this dialogue on aesthetics the question has arisen as to whether Shelley had first had a "good idea" to versify or whether his idea and his words were organically joined. Although Shelley's actual method cannot be determined, Hopkins' preference is perfectly clear.

> In writing this poem Shelley must either have put before his mind an idea which he wishes to embody in words . . . or else the idea rose in the forms of expression which we read in the poem in his mind, thought and expression indistinguishable. The latter I believe to be the truer way of regarding composition. (*J*, 109–10)

Hopkins' "modernity" (or if this word is repellent, his "attractiveness to the modern sensibility") lies in his probing attitude toward language, which is manifest in his early journals and diaries and which continues throughout his later career. The other central characteristic that has made him congenial to the modern mind is what can only be termed—perhaps tritely—his "tortured personality." Almost all critics of Hopkins deal in one way or another with his unique treatment of language and with the much-discussed dichotomies of his private life: poet vs. priest; faith vs. doubt; celebrant of Nature vs. prophet of suffering, and the like.

I believe that Hopkins' language and his private conflicts are more intimately related than has hitherto been thought. As with Arnold, the nub of the problem is epistemology. Also, as with Arnold, an analogy illuminates Hopkins' use of language, his life, and the meanings of his poetry. The analogy, as we might suspect for Hopkins, is theological. Hopkins' problem, unlike that of many of his contemporaries, is not a conflict between belief and unbelief; it is a conflict between two possible modes of believing: belief in a transcendent vs. an immanent God. Although the Christian God is traditionally conceived as being both transcendent and immanent, the

91

polar extremes of the conflict represent positions outside Christianity: deism and pantheism.

It is clear that the new modes of thought of the seventeenth century helped to bring about a theological corollary: deism. If reality was "out there," independent of human formulation, it followed that God also was "out there" or "up there," remote and independent of cove- nantal relations with His people. He became the gifted Artisan who constructed the intricate machinery of the universe. He was no more a part of the inner life of His creation than a jeweler was a part of a clock he had designed. The 19th Psalm's deeply human exultation in the personal Ruler of the universe, who made the sun like a bridegroom, was converted by Addison to the cool, reasoned craftsmanship of the deist cosmos.

> What though in solemn silence all
> Move round the dark terrestial ball;
> What though nor real voice nor sound
> Amid their radiant orbs be found;
> In reason's ear they all rejoice,
> And utter forth a glorious voice;
> Forever singing as they shine,
> "The hand that made us is Divine."

Impressive as Addison's powerful lines are, they reflect neither the passion of the Hebrew poet nor the human warmth of Jesus of Nazareth. The external, "given" God whom we know only by the works of His hand is very close to Blake's Nobodaddy.

I believe, following the suggestions of modern theologians like Paul Tillich or Dietrich Bonhoeffer, that "orthodox" nineteenth-century Christianity—both Catholic and Protestant—tended toward deism. Based firmly upon Paley's *Evidences* and a belief in the literal and "factual" truth of the Scriptures, early Victorian Christianity, like early Victorian science, worshipped an external reality, a fixed order that was independent of human creativity. Protestant insistence on a rigid reliance on the word of Scripture and tractarian insistence on dogma, preserved in purity from the patristic age, both betray an externalized theory of knowledge. The divine Old Man who presided over Victorian legalism and who served either as a definable rock of refuge for the countless conversions that filled the pages of Victorian memoirs or as a definable concept to be rejected by the honest doubters who filled the pages of other Victorian memoirs, surely bears a striking resemblance to the God of deism. Popular orthodoxy suffered from the same ills that beset aesthetics in the eighteenth century. Creeds, dogmas, and Scripture were often regarded as a mirror of God rather than as a creative analogy for Him. The imaginative rebellions in theology both within and without Christianity in the nineteenth century were rebellions against a tendency in established Christianity toward the fixed and externalist system so common in deism. The theological writing and poetry of Blake, Wordsworth, Coleridge, and Carlyle—among English literary figures—come immediately to mind and the works of German romantic idealists—Kant, Goethe, and Nietzsche.

In Gerard Manley Hopkins, more than in almost any other nineteenth-century figure, we can see sharply focused not only the nineteenth-century poet's struggle with words and things, but also the nineteenth-century theologian's struggle with deism. As so many of Hopkins' poems and other writings show, he was deeply moved by a vision of God's immanence in nature. His admiration for Wordsworth's "Intimations Ode" indicates his recognition of the older poet's new sense of divine immanence. Hopkins wrote Dixon in 1886 that "in Wordsworth when he wrote that ode human nature got another of those shocks, and the tremble from it is spreading."[3]

3. From *The Correspondence of Gerard Manley Hopkins and Richard Watson Dixon*, Claude Colleer Abbott, ed. (London, published by the Oxford University Press by arrangement with the Society of Jesus, 1955), 148. Hereafter cited as *Correspondence*. See also David A. Downes's excellent discussion of Hopkins' romanticism in *Victorian Portraits: Hopkins and Pater* (New York, Bookman Associates, 1965), 84–101.

Yet, he was just as deeply committed to Christian orthodoxy, first Anglican, then Roman Catholic. His orthodoxy, as his letters, sermons, and other spiritual writings indicate, was closely aligned to the established Christianity that was oriented toward a rigidly objective theology. Hopkins' vision of God in nature, his sense of God within the self, his Tillichian description of God as "the ground of being" in "The Wreck of the Deutschland," all indicate the poet's deep dissatisfaction with the system of thought so general in the eighteenth and nineteenth centuries. Yet his compulsive commitment to nineteenth-century orthodoxy, precisely defined, created a conflict in his personal life and in his art. This is not the simple pattern, so often discussed, of doubt vs. faith or, in Hopkins' case, priest vs. poet. Instead, it is a complex problem that involves a difficult theological conflict *within* the context of Christianity on the one hand and a difficult aesthetic conflict on the other.

At the risk of overschematizing, I should like to consider the double development and articulation of Hopkins' conflicts—theological and artistic—chronologically, within the common formulation of his career into three periods. In each period he wrestled with his conflicts in a different way. The early poems of the intense young Oxonian register a rigid Anglican orthodoxy, interspersed with the terror that commonly accompanies an externalist theology: why is God absent? what if He is dead? The mature nature poems of his middle period, beginning with "The Wreck of the Deutschland," reflect an immanentist, sacramental vision of God, nature, and man. God is not absent or remotely above His creation; instead, He is the ground of being and the natural world is "charged" with His glory. If these two periods may be seen as representing the poles of the theological dichotomy, Hopkins' last period—the time of the sonnets of desolation—may be seen as the period of raw and terrifying conflict, not between doubt and faith, but between two kinds of faith: Victorian orthodoxy and the immanentist, incarnational Christianity so germane both

to Hopkins' religious sensibility and to his creative imagination as a poet. It is no longer sufficient to explain
Hopkins through the medieval theological perspectives of
Thomas Aquinas or Duns Scotus. Medieval philosophy is
important in understanding Hopkins, but we must keep
in mind that he was a modern, not a medieval man; John
Locke had intervened. Victorian orthodoxy and medieval
Catholicism are not convertible terms. Hopkins' evolving
recognition of this fact produced his personal tensions
and generated his most powerful poetry. His theological
and his artistic debates are analogous and serve as brilliant
examples of the development of language, poetry, and
Christianity in the modern world. All three were and are
in crisis.

Consolation

THE POWERLESS POET

Acknowledgment of the spreading decay of an objective world view on the part of nineteenth-century poets has become a critical commonplace. This loss of faith,
as Robert Langbaum has pointed out, caused the nineteenth century to produce a poetry based on individual
experience rather than on dogmatic system.

Hopkins' biography and poems provide a contrast.
In an age of religious doubt and uncertainty, when it
seemed to most intellectuals that the traditional Christian world view was collapsing, Hopkins became a Jesuit
and devoted his life and his art to the service of the
Roman Catholic Church. His works express a clearly formulated, objective view of the world that other Victorian
poets lacked. If his letters and poetry sometimes indicate
unhappiness and wrenching personal tensions, they never
indicate an intellectual doubt of his religious position. He
seems never to have undergone a crisis in faith similar to
those chronicled in *In Memoriam* or "Dover Beach." He
clung instead to the spar of faith in the flood of doubt,
not only with tenacity, but with apparent confidence.
The systematic Catholic theology that, for many Victorians, had collapsed, attracted not only Hopkins' accep-

tance but became the subject of his poetry. Hopkins was no romantic medievalist toying with Catholicism for its aesthetic values, like Morris, Rossetti, Wilde, or Pater. His early training was in the ascetic Anglo-Catholicism of Pusey and Liddon, and he was received into the Roman Catholic Church by the austere Newman himself.

Although Hopkins—even in his blackest moods—never suggested the possibility of giving up belief in God or abandoning Christianity, it is obvious that he had, like Newman, if not doubts, enormous difficulties. His difficulties, unlike those of so many Victorians, were within the framework of Christianity. This fact does not make them less serious; for Hopkins, the committed priest, they became even more traumatic. Pusey, Liddon—and even Newman—were precisely the trouble. Hopkins' initial faith—the religion of the severe Oxonian of 1863–1866 —was an acceptance of the given. His faith was not so much a state of mind and heart in relation to God, as Saint Paul described the virtue, but was a faith in the proposition of God and in a sharply defined dogmatic scheme. It was, I would suggest, Catholicism deistically understood. Like so much Victorian orthodoxy (including the Evangelicalism of the 1860s), Hopkins' faith, although maintained with deep emotional intensity, was directed to a system of intellectual beliefs external to himself. The tractarian attempt to define and verbalize the theological and historical basis for Christianity found an apt pupil in Hopkins. Keble's choice of words in describing the "deposit of faith" as a jewel preserved by the Fathers and guarded by the Church of England helped condition Hopkins' attitude. Although the sacramentalism of both tractarians and Roman Catholics provided a broad qualification of the deist tendencies of their orthodoxy, it was not always enough.

Examining some of Hopkins' early poems, written between 1862 and his conversion in 1866, will perhaps shed light on the conflict raised for intelligent and sensitive Victorian Christians. The first poem I discuss does not deal with theology at all, yet the state of mind it

GERARD MANLEY HOPKINS

implies may be regarded as analogous to Hopkins' religious difficulties during these years.

"The Alchemist in the City," dated May, 1865, dramatizes a state of mind not uncommon among nineteenth-century poets—impotent passivity. The poem is a dramatic monologue, delivered by an unsuccessful alchemist, who is trapped in the midst of a world that goes on about him but with which he is unable to communicate and in which he is unable to take part.

> My window shows the travelling clouds,
> Leaves spent, new seasons, alter'd sky,
> The making and the melting crowds:
> The whole world passes; I stand by.[4]

The situation, with less intensity, is quite similar to that of the late sonnets of desolation. The speaker is isolated from the world about him and is unable to act. The creativity of the alchemist, a symbolic agent of transformation, has been paralyzed and stifled. He is conscious that he has been wasting his "meted hours" in solitary effort while others have had "happy promises fulfill'd." Time has now intervened to render impossible the alchemist's discovery of a process to make gold.

> But now before the pot can glow
> With not to be discover'd gold,
> At length the bellows shall not blow,
> The furnace shall at last be cold.

Even more distressing is the recognition that his years of isolation have made resumption of normal intercourse with others in the community as impossible as age has rendered continuation of the lonely dedication of the alchemist.

4. All quotations from Hopkins' poems are from *The Poems of Gerard Manley Hopkins*, W.H. Gardner and N.H. Mackenzie, eds., 4th ed. (London, published by the Oxford University Press by arrangement with the Society of Jesus, 1967). Hereafter cited as *P*.

Yet it is now too late to heal
The incapable and cumbrous shame
Which makes me when with men I deal
More powerless than the blind or lame.

The speaker of the poem comes to the conclusion that he desires neither the active life of the city around him nor the anxious and unsuccessful search into his "thankless lore." Instead, he yearns for the "wilderness." This feeling comes to him most strongly in the evening or morning when he looks out toward a spot on the horizon and hungers "to be there."

Then sweetest seems the houseless shore,
Then free and kind the wilderness.

Or ancient mounds that cover bones,
Or rocks where rockdoves do repair
And trees of terebinth and stones
And silence and a gulf of air.

In frustration at his inability either to transform base metal to gold or to engage in the active life of the community, the speaker turns with relief and longing to images of quietude, passivity, and death. His central desire is to lie on a height in that quiet wilderness after sunset

And pierce the yellow waxen light
With free long looking, ere I die.

Although "The Alchemist in the City" does not deal directly with religious problems, the relationship is clear. Its theme is quite similar to those we have seen in Matthew Arnold's works. The creative artist (artisan in this case) is unable to make any meaningful contact outside himself. Like Empedocles, he feels himself an alien in the city and a failure in his art. Since he is unable to create or transform, he must passively accept the terms of nature. A theological parallel is that the universe is a fixed mechanism, designed by a mysterious designer who "lives, alas, away"; the speaker of the poem, at any rate, fails in establishing any relation with Him. The wilderness of this poem is unlike the nature of

"Tintern Abbey." Its outstanding features are ancient mounds that cover bones, rocks,

> And trees of terebinth and stones
> And silence and a gulf of air.

At best, it is like the wilderness into which Moses led the children of Israel—without, in this case, a guiding pillar of cloud or fire.

In a poem written two months later, September, 1865, Hopkins described a situation similar to that of the alchemist, this time specifically in religious terms, though in terms of struggle rather than passivity. The poem, No. 18 in Gardner's fourth edition, deals with a traditional problem of the practicing Christian: the difficulty of prayer. The speaker, like Hamlet's uncle, feels that his prayers are not reaching God.

> My prayers must meet a brazen heaven
> And fail or scatter all away.
> Unclean and seeming unforgiven
> My prayers I scarcely call to pray.
> I cannot buoy my heart above;
> Above it cannot entrance win.
> I reckon precedents of love,
> But feel the long success of sin.

Although this poem must be considered squarely in the tradition of Christian devotional verse, this fact does not change its apparent distress or alter the situation of its speaker, who is struggling to reach a far-away God, who lives "above." His prayers strike unyielding brass and fall away. As William Blake might have told him, Nobodaddy is well known for his deaf ear.

A month later Hopkins wrote a poem that once more emphasized God's distance and His separation from human concerns, but suggested a remedy: the sacrament. "The Half-way House" opens with the speaker's sense that God is still "above" and that there can be no relationship between God and man unless He will "come down."

Love I was shewn upon the mountain-side
And bid to catch Him ere the drop of day.
See, Love, I creep and Thou on wings dost ride:
Love, it is evening now and Thou away,
Love, it grows darker here and Thou art above;
Love, come down to me if Thy name be Love.

In the last stanza of this poem is the paradox that throughout Hopkins' career created spiritual tension. It is impossible to love an abstract God who is remote and "above." He must be seen and realized in some way upon earth. A metaphysical First Cause is not a fit object for human love; it is incapable of maintaining a personal relationship.

Hear yet my paradox: Love, when all is given,
To see Thee I must see Thee, to love, love;
I must o'ertake Thee at once and under heaven
If I shall overtake Thee at last above.

These lines reflect traditional incarnational theology. God is to be found in a man, Christ; He must be found in the midst of human life if He is to be found at all. The closing couplet of the poem, reminiscent of George Herbert, suggests the Holy Communion as the physical mode of knowing God. As Christ appeared physically to the disciples at Emmaus (Luke 23 : 13 ff.), so He appears to the Christian in the sacrament.

You have your wish; enter these walls, one said:
He is with you in the breaking of the bread.

Hopkins' sacramentalism was surely one of the strongest motivations for his conversion to Roman Catholicism. It was the foundation of his religious life, as he said in an early letter to his father.[5] Ironically, it was this very sacramentalism that later caused him difficulty.

5. *Further Letters of Gerard Manley Hopkins*, Claude Colleer Abbott, 2d ed. (London, Oxford University Press, 1956), 92.

In January of 1866 Hopkins wrote "The Habit of Perfection." This perceptive metaphysical poem is devoted to an elaborate denial of the senses in favor of a spiritual choice of God. It is based on one of the central traditions of Christian devotion: the renunciation of images. Hearing, for instance, is to be relinquished for an "elected silence." The eyes are to "be shelled . . . with double dark [to] find the uncreated light." The assumptions here are quite opposite from those of "The Half-way House." God, it is certain, is not to be found in ordinary human life, but only in a metaphysical beyond, for which the senses are a poor analogy.

> O feel-of-primrose hands, O feet
> That want the yield of plushy sward,
> But you shall walk the golden street
> And you unhouse and house the Lord.
>
> And, Poverty, be thou the bride
> And now the marriage feast begun,
> And lily-coloured clothes provide
> Your spouse not laboured-at nor spun.

Although there is nothing in "The Habit of Perfection" that is not in traditional Christian devotional material, its severe metaphysical asceticism contrasts sharply with the other side of Hopkins' nature and his theology. The conflict becomes only too clear when the prayers for elected silence and double dark are answered during the time of the "terrible sonnets." We see also Hopkins' characteristic inner strife in the paradoxically sensual mode of rendering an ascetic theme.

"Nondum," a questioning poem addressed to Isaiah's hidden God, was written sometime during Lent of 1866, only a few months before Hopkins' reception into the Roman Catholic Church. Here is more fully realized than in any of Hopkins' other poetry—except the terrible sonnets—what J. Hillis Miller has called "the disappearance of God." No matter how loudly human beings call, there is no answer.

God, though to Thee our psalm we raise
No answering voice comes from the skies;
To Thee the trembling sinner prays
But no forgiving voice replies;
Our prayer seems lost in desert ways,
Our hymn in the vast silence dies.

The elaborate design celebrated by Addison in his adaptation of the 19th Psalm is not exhilarating; it is terrifying. The hand that formed the universe may be divine, but it cannot be found.

We see the glories of the earth
But not the hand that wrought them all:
Night to a myriad worlds gives birth,
Yet like a lighted empty hall
Where stands no host at door or hearth
Vacant creation's lamps appal.

After noting the "unbroken silence" of the ages and considering the terrifying "abysses infinite," Hopkins closed this poem with a Tennysonian analogy, strongly reminiscent of the lost-child simile of Section LIV of *In Memoriam* and its resolution in Section CXXIV:

Oh! till Thou givest that sense beyond,
To show Thee that Thou art, and near,
Let patience with her chastening wand
Dispel the doubt and dry the tear;
And lead me child-like by the hand
If still in darkness not in fear.

Speak! whisper to my watching heart
One word—as when a mother speaks
Soft, when she sees her infant start,
Till dimpled joy steals o'er its cheeks.
Then, to behold Thee as Thou art,
I'll wait till morn eternal breaks.

We have, then, in these five early poems, which immediately preceded Hopkins' conversion, a kind of prelude to the sonnets of desolation, which came nearly twenty years later. Although the atmosphere of the earlier poems has not reached the intensity of the "terrible crystal," which so horrified Canon Dixon in later years, the situation is quite similar. The speaker finds himself alone in a universe from which God has disappeared. The world is not, in Hopkins' later phrase, "news of God." It is instead His mechanical construct. God may indeed exist, but only as a metaphysical abstraction. He is "above"; man is below. Like the alchemist in the city, the speaker is without the power of transformation. God's mysterious transcendence and separation from the world leave an appalling vacancy. Although Saint John had described God as the Word, the Word that was made flesh and dwelt among us, now both God and man are incommunicado. The problem is not so much that Hopkins doubts the existence of God, or even the formal Christian statements of faith. The problem is that he cannot relate these abstract formulations to his own inner experience. This is, I believe, the deist dilemma or, to be precise, the dilemma of a Christian who is attempting to come to grips with Christianity through a deist theory of knowledge. If God is only "out there," and is to be known only by external observation of His works, what happens when observation or experience fails to reveal Him? The answer is to be found in the agony of nineteenth-century doubting.

GROUND OF BEING AND GROUND OF KNOWLEDGE

The record of Hopkins' first attempt at a solution of his theological and epistemological quandary is to be found in another group of early poems characterized by a far different use of words and symbols. I refer to those poems related to his compelling interest in the sea. His journals teem with careful descriptions of the sea. The journal for August, 1872, for instance, contains four pages of observation of the sea, noted during a vacation on the

Isle of Man.[6] But far more revealing than this fascination with the sea is Hopkins' youthful interest in mermaids, following the pattern of Tennyson and Arnold. In 1862, when he was eighteen, Hopkins wrote his erotic and evocative "A Vision of the Mermaids." In 1864 at Oxford he wrote his sea poem "Rest," the first two verses of which were changed to "Heaven-Haven." Shortly thereafter Hopkins became interested enough in Garnett's "The Nix" to use it as the chief example in his essay on aesthetics, "On the Origin of Beauty," and to write a seven-stanza continuation of it, which was not published with the rest of his poetry until the recent fourth edition. These three early poems and "The Wreck of the Deutschland," with which Hopkins opened his career, reflect the early conflict I have just described and represent his attempts to solve it. The sea symbolism of these four poems, like that of Tennyson or Arnold, follows a recognizable pattern of development. These early sea poems present a conflict—personal, theological, and artistic —that parallels Hopkins' process of conversion to the Roman Catholic Church and, significantly, the seven-year hiatus in his artistic career. Evidently, the conflict was reconciled and transformed, as indicated by the mature development expressed in "The Wreck of the Deutschland." Through the symbol of the sea Hopkins was able to find, on the one hand, the artistic means to reconcile experience and Christian dogma in poetry and, on the other, the psychological means to release the energy and direct the will to begin his poetic career.

*　　*　　*　　*

"Whoever looks into the water," Jung has written, "sees his own image, but behind it living creatures soon loom up; fishes, presumably, harmless dwellers of the deep—harmless, if only the lake were not haunted. They are water beings of a peculiar sort. Sometimes a nixie

6. *J.*, 222–25.

gets into the fisherman's net, a female, half-human fish."[7] Whether nixies, sirens, and mermaids are versions of the *anima*, as Jung suggests, there can be no doubt that the youthful Hopkins, like Tennyson and Arnold, caught some in his net. "A Vision of the Mermaids," with its Keatsian and Tennysonian overtones, tells of mermaids "Ris'n from the deeps to gaze on sun and heaven." A striking sexual metaphor describes their crowding like blown flowers around the rock upon which the speaker sits.

> Soon—as when Summer of his sister Spring
> Crushes and tears the rare enjewelling,
> And boasting "I have fairer things than these"
> Plashes amidst the billowy apple-trees
> His lusty hands, in gusts of scented wind
> Swirling out bloom till all the air is blind
> With rosy foam and pelting blossom and mists
> Of driving vermeil-rain; and, as he lists,
> The dainty onyx-coronals deflowers,
> A glorious wanton; . . .

Although the mermaids sport, "careless" of the speaker, the erotic and aesthetic pleasure of the scene is marred, as it is in the sea pictures of Tennyson and Arnold.

> And a sweet sadness dwelt on everyone;
> I knew not why,—but know that sadness dwells
> On Mermaids—whether that they ring the knells
> Of seamen whelm'd in chasms of the mid-main,
> As poets sing; or that it is a pain
> To know the dusk depths of the ponderous sea,
> The miles profound of solid green, and be
> With loath'd cold fishes, far from man—or what;—
> I know the sadness but the cause know not.

7. *Archetypes of the Collective Unconscious* in *The Basic Writings of C.G. Jung,* Violet Staub·de Laszlo, ed. (New York, Modern Library, 1959), 308, 309.

Here, as in Tennyson's "The Mermaid" or Arnold's "The Forsaken Merman," we have intimations of the mysterious, alien beauty of the depths. The mermaids are alluring, yet possessed of a painful and perhaps dangerous knowledge, "the dusk depths of the ponderous sea." The vision is drowned at sunset by the incoming tide, which apparently "whelms" the mermaids as it did the seamen.

> A stealthy wind crept round seeking to blow,
> Linger'd, then raised the washing waves and drench'd
> The floating blooms and with tide flowing quench'd
> The rosy isles. . . .

The speaker withdraws to escape the rising water and watches with poignant thoughts as the sea covers the vantage point from which he had observed the enticing mermaids.

> White loom'd my rock, the water gurgling o'er,
> Whence oft I watch but see those Mermaids now no more.

The plaintive sadness of the mermaids' song affects the speaker, and the poem closes with a sense of yearning emptiness. The speaker is attracted to the beauty of the sea world, but he is fearful of its strangeness, its lonely immensities, and the danger sea knowledge may bring. The isolation of the speaker on his solitary rock, forever sundered from the sea, reminds one of the stranded speaker of "Dover Beach" or the powerless alchemist.

The forbidding yet compelling quality of the sea is even more pronounced in Hopkins' early poem "Rest," which implies an inner tension that is outwardly expressed by the poet's ambivalent attitude toward the sea. First appearing in a diary of 1864, "Rest" concerns a person who is torn between two attitudes toward the sea, much as the speaker of the Old English "Sea-Farer." The opening stanzas show an affinity to Tennyson's "Lotos-Eaters" in their desire for peace, away from the dangers of the cruel sea.

I have desired to go
Where springs not fail;
To fields where flies not the unbridled hail,
And a few lilies blow.
I have desired to be
Where havens are dumb;
Where the green water-heads may never come,
As in the unloved sea.

or

I have desired to be
Where gales not come;
Where the green swell is in the havens dumb
And sundered from the sea.

As in the earlier "Vision of the Mermaids," the ocean is
alien, "unloved," and the speaker, like the speaker of "A
Vision," is "sunder'd from the sea"—or at least, he hopes
to be. The passivity of this desire for peace is paralleled
by dozens of tractarian poems, whose authors have fled
worldly engagement for the supposed stability of the
Church. Yet this hope for rest, safety—a static security
away from the dangerous sea knowledge—is modified by
a compulsion to undertake a sea quest in the second half
of the poem.

I must hunt down the prize
Where my heart lists.
Must see the eagle's bulk, render'd in mists,
Hang of a treble size.
Must see the waters roll
Where seas set
Towards wastes where round the ice-blocks tilt and fret
Not so far from the pole

In these lines from Hopkins' early diary we find the need
to "hunt down a prize" on the farthest reaches of the
ocean—a prize hidden somewhere among wastes and
mists. In contrast to the earlier lines, which asked for
passive "being" in silent harbors, there is now a desire to
hunt and to see. The dialectic of the poem reminds us of

Tennyson's ambiguous night journey in which Ulysses yearns "in desire / To follow knowledge like a sinking star, / Beyond the utmost bound of human thought."

Hopkins' last sea poem before his conversion returned to the mermaid theme. Richard Garnett's "The Nix" is a ballad related to the many tales of mermaids, nixies, neckans, and so on, who lure young girls or young men to the depths. In this poem, the speaker is a girl whose beauty has been envied by a nix.

> The crafty Nix, more false than fair,
> Whose haunt in arrowy Iser lies.
> She envied me my golden hair.
> She envied me my azure eyes.

The nix lures the girl "to her crystal grot" and there exchanges magically her physical appearance for the girl's. "Her locks of jet, her eyes of flame / Were mine, and hers my semblance fair." Although the speaker pleads with the nix to restore her looks,

> She smiles in scorn, she disappears,
> And here I sit and see no sun,
> My eyes of fire are quenched in tears,
> And all my darksome locks undone.

With these lines Garnett's poem ends. In Hopkins' continuation, the nix (now with the blue eyes and blond hair of the girl) practices her wiles on the speaker's lover Fabian.

> He sees her, O but he must miss
> A something in her face of guile,
> And relish not her loveless kiss
> And wonder at her shallow smile.

The only one who can help the girl regain her yellow hair and blue eyes is a witch who lives on "the bored and bitten rocks / Not so far outward in the sea." The girl, however, is afraid of undertaking a sea journey and is also afraid of the consequences on land if she does so. Hopkins' portion of the poem ends in the unresolved tension of the following stanzas.

Alas! but I am all at fault,
Nor locks nor eyes shall win again.
I dare not taste the thickening salt,
I cannot meet the swallowing main.

Or if I go, she stays meanwhile,
Who means to wed or means to kill,
And speeds uncheck'd her murderous guile
Or wholly winds him to her will.

Hopkins' addition is revealing. He changed a poem that was essentially finished and resolved (though unhappily) to an unresolved mental struggle. Here we have a supernatural creature of the sea, a nix, who is capable of robbing one of one's identity through magic transformation. In Hopkins' addition, powers associated with the sea are also capable of a retransformation back to one's true identity—but at the cost of conquering one's fear of the sea by meeting "the swallowing main," by entrusting oneself to the sea-witch who can make the transformation. The dilemma is similar to that of "A Vision" and "Rest": Does the speaker dare to go to sea or not?

The psychic conflict expressed in these early poems through the evocative symbol of the sea is in some ways equivalent to those mirrored in certain of Tennyson's and Arnold's early poems, say "The Hesperides" or "The Forsaken Merman." I believe that this conflict is a significant cause of the much-discussed hiatus in Hopkins' artistic career, following his entry into the Society of Jesus. Theologically, Hopkins had to decide whether God was only transcendent, only above, and separate from His creation or whether He was immanent in it, to be known in the heart of man through the phenomena of the universe. On a personal level the question for Hopkins was how to keep his identity as a Jesuit and still venture into the beautiful yet dangerous world of art, how to keep the identity of his stable dogmatic belief and still risk it on the ever-moving ocean of experience. Ten years elapsed after the writing of "The Nix" before Hopkins could reconcile these dilemmas. His solution came fittingly in the gigantic ocean rhythms of "The Wreck of the Deutschland." The answers yielded by the sea in "The Wreck" are the answers of the Christian Gospel: One must lose one's identity to gain it; one must test one's belief to keep it; God is to be found not only "above," but also in the depths.

*   *   *   *

Most critics would agree that one theme of "The Wreck of the Deutschland" is the paradox of God's mercy and His mastery. The poem attempts to answer the classic question: How can a merciful God inflict pain and death on His creatures? In the archetypal and complexly ambivalent symbol of the sea Hopkins found a parallel to the two aspects of God: the merciful Father versus the stern and terrifying Master of the universe. But there is another and perhaps more interesting paradox in the poem, also expressed through water imagery, that relates Hopkins to the subjective, experiential attitudes of his age while it attempts to retain the systematic theological orthodoxy so important to a Jesuit poet. This added paradox I take to be the external power of God, buffeting and mastering man from without, as opposed to the internal, indwelling grace of God that transforms him to a different person, that in fact gives him divine characteristics, makes him act

> in God's eye what in God's eye he is—
> Christ—for Christ plays in ten thousand places,
> Lovely in limbs, and lovely in eyes not his
> To the Father through the features of men's faces.

The recognition of God's immanence in the universe and in man himself is related to a renewed faith in the power of the creative imagination. The profound meaning of "The Wreck of the Deutschland" is found, then, in the tension between God acting externally through the storm of the elements and God acting internally through the

110

fluid entry of grace into the soul. Although man is struck with "an anvil–ding," God's will is forged with "fire in him." God may come "at once, as once at a crash Paul, / Or as Austin, a lingering-out sweet skill." Although Hopkins, unlike many of his contemporaries, held certain dogmatic statements about God to be factually and objectively true, their significance in the poem is always experienced internally. Hopkins was not interested in the formal definitions of the theologian. Instead, he attempted to create symbols through which God can actually be known. His method in "The Wreck" was not to make statements about the attributes of God, but to explore their effects on his own heart and the heart of a drowning nun. Only in the ocean could Hopkins find a symbol immense and sweeping enough to join both the external and internal manifestations of God and to unite them with the inner experience of man.

The poem opens powerfully with a symbolic identification of God and the sea. God is described in the first stanza with a series of three appositives:

> God! giver of breath and bread;
> World's strand, sway of the sea;
> Lord of living and dead.

The metaphor of God as sand and water, shore and ocean, is an important key to our understanding of the poem, and it is repeated several times. In the opening lines it brings together in a kind of prologue to the poem the paradox that will develop. God is both the finite, objective, and stationary shore (as Christ takes on the finite nature of man through the Incarnation) and the infinite, eternal, yet moving sea—a sea that so often in the nineteenth century served to symbolize not only God but the "divine" depths of man, created in God's image. The passengers of the *Deutschland* meet God by striking "the combs of a smother of sand" in the ocean. "The goal was a shoal, of a fourth the doom to be drowned."

The metaphor of sand and water is continued in Stanza 4, but here it is skillfully modified to apply to the

111

condition of man and to establish a symbolic relation between man and God.

> I am soft sift
> In an hourglass—at the wall
> Fast, but mined with a motion, a drift,
> And it crowds and it combs to the fall;
> I steady as a water in a well, to a poise, to a pane,
> But roped with, always, all the way down from the tall
> Fells or flanks of the voel, a vein
> Of the gospel proffer, a pressure, a principle, Christ's gift.

Here the sand implies mutability and death. Man's impermanence is "a motion, a drift," as the sand "crowds and it combs to the fall." The word "combs" anticipates another monument to man's impermanence, "the combs of a smother of sand" where the ship is drawn "Dead to the Kentish Knock." Still, Stanza 4 offers an image of hope to counteract the downward running sands of the hourglass; man can also be viewed not as impermanent, always falling, but "steady as a water in a well." The steadiness of the water within the well is made possible only by the stream of water from the heights to which it is "roped," just as the heart within man is kept "steady" by the "vein / Of the gospel proffer . . . Christ's gift." The image of water filling a well is connected in Stanza 7 to the swelling of the "high flood," to the gushing, flushing, and brimming of Stanza 8, and finally, in the closing prayer of the poem, addressed to the "Dame, at our door / Drowned." Even here, the water–sand imagery is continued, for the nun is "Drowned, and among our shoals." It is also apparent that Hopkins' water imagery here is related to the fountain symbolism so characteristic of romantic aesthetics. Man's time on earth may be mutable, but he is not cut off from God in a mechanical universe.

The objective fact of the Incarnation is stressed in Stanzas 6, 7, and 8. When Hopkins expressed this dogmatic summary of his belief through the image of moving water, however, he related it to universal human experience. God's mystery, his "stress and his stroke," come not "out of his bliss," "Nor first from heaven," but from the fact of the Incarnation. Divine power is not only "above," but it rises out of the human situation, as exemplified in the life of the man Jesus. Through the image of the river,[8] which ultimately joins the sea (as the stream of Stanza 4 joins the well), Hopkins united the time-bound, finite condition of man to the infinite and eternal person of God, the God who entered man's situation in the Incarnation. It is the Incarnation "That guilt is hushed by, hearts are flushed by and melt"; it "rides time like riding a river." Not only is the mystery infinite and eternal, but it is directly related to man in time and originates in human action and creativity.

> It dates from day
> Of his going in Galilee;
> Warm-laid grave of a womb-life grey;
> Manger, maiden's knee;
> The dense and the driven Passion, and frightful sweat:
> Thence the discharge of it, there its swelling to be,
> Though felt before, though in high flood yet—
> What none would have known of it, only the heart, being
> hard at bay. . . .

Only direct human experience at its deepest—"the heart, being hard at bay"—can know the truth about God. Only the human life of Christ "Is out with it!" The deist dilemma evaporates in the face of the central doctrine of Christianity. God's power (His "stroke dealt") does not come "first from heaven." It is not only found in the impressive majesty of the external universe, exemplified

---

8. John Keating interprets the river as "the indifference and irreligion that stream through history," in *The Wreck of the Deutschland: An Essay and Commentary* (Kent, Ohio, Kent State University Press, 1963), 64. This view seems to me untenable, in the light of the images of flushing, melting, discharging, swelling, and flooding, that all refer to the mystery of the Incarnation of Christ.

by "stars and storms" here, or the majestic progression of the spheres in Addison's rendering; it rises also from the heart of a man. "It rides time." Hopkins' recognition of the rigidity of the nineteenth-century orthodoxy that intensified his own doubts is reflected in the last line of Stanza 6: "And here the faithful waver, the faithless fable and miss."

In Stanza 8, experiencing the full reality of "the hero of Calvary" is likened to biting into a "lush-kept plush-capped sloe." The imagery is still consonant with the river-and-well imagery of the preceding stanzas. The sloe will "Gush!—flush the man, the being with it, sour or sweet, / Brim, in a flash, full!" In the image of brimming full Hopkins anticipated the surrender of the nun to drowning and the filling of man with Christ's Spirit, the Holy Ghost.

Stanza 13 is a terrifying, onomatopoeic description of the storm wind rising over the ocean deeps.

> And the sea flint-flake, black-backed in the regular blow,
> Sitting Eastnortheast, in cursed quarter, the wind;
> Wiry and white-fiery and whirlwind-swivellèd snow
> Spins to the widow-making unchilding unfathering deeps.

Here Hopkins pictured an unknown, mastering God through the images of the sea and whirlwind. Besides the reference to the whirlwind of the Book of Job, there is another biblical reference in the last line of the stanza that once more identifies the sea as God and enriches the complexity of its symbolism by allusion. Not only does the phrase, "widow-making unchilding unfathering deeps," suggest the strange loneliness of the mermaids' "ponderous sea," but it also relates the ocean to the words of Christ: "He that loveth father or mother more than me is not worthy of me: and he that loveth son or daughter more than me is not worthy of me" (Matthew 10 : 37). These words of Christ had a special relevance for Hopkins and the five nuns as well, who gave up family and friends to enter the religious life.

After the *Deutschland* strikes the "smother of

sand," it is clear that God Himself is responsible for "washing away" the lives.

> They fought with God's cold—
> And they could not and fell to the deck
> (Crushed them) or water (and drowned them) or
>   rolled
> With the sea-romp over the wreck.

Yet the tall nun's calling over the tumult touches the heart of the poet in its "bower of bone," and again the relation between God and man—in this case the poet—is established by the symbol of water. God's washing away of the lives in the storm arouses a response of washing, melting tears in the heart of the poet. "Why, tears! is it? tears; such a melting, a madrigal start! / Never-eldering revel and river of youth, . . ." Similarly, the waves of "rash smart sloggering brine" blind the nun, yet paradoxically allow her to see one thing, to have "one fetch in her" (to use Hopkins' wave metaphor): The stormy waves outside call forth a responding wave from within—the external battering of God evokes her internal vision of Christ. God is seen as the transcendent, pursuing hunter, the "Orion of light," the "martyr-master," but He is also the wild water in which the nuns are "sisterly sealed, . . . To bathe in his fall-gold mercies."

In Stanza 25 the poet ponders the meaning of the tall nun's cry for Christ.

> The majesty! what did she mean?
> Breathe, arch and original Breath.
> Is it love in her of the being as her lover had been?
> Breathe, body of lovely Death.

Did the nun call for death because Christ, her lover, had also died? Is the nun, like Whitman in "Out of the Cradle," yearning for death with a nearly erotic desire? The next lines deny this possibility. Even Christ's disciples had no such death wish. "They were else-minded then, altogether, the men / Woke thee with a *We are perishing* in the weather of Gennesareth." The nun was not neurotically in love with death, nor was she calling for "the crown" or "for ease." Instead she was offering herself in total surrender to Christ.

> . . . There then! the Master,
> *Ipse*, the only one, Christ, King, Head:
> He was to cure the extremity where he had cast her;
>   Do, deal, lord it with living and dead;
> Let him ride, her pride, in his triumph, despatch and have done
>   with his doom there.

Although the image of Christ the King riding in His triumph reminds us of the Palm Sunday entry into Jerusalem, this passage also hints at the spiritual consummation of the marriage between Christ and His bride. This sexual aspect of the imagery is clear in Stanza 30, in which the nun is connected with the Virgin Mary, who conceived Jesus by the Holy Ghost.

> Jesu, heart's light,
> Jesu, maid's son,
> What was the feast followed the night
>   Thou hadst glory of this nun?—
> Feast of the one woman without stain.
> For so conceivèd, so to conceive thee is done;
>   But here was heart-throe, birth of a brain,
> Word, that heard and kept thee and uttered thee outright.

The feast that followed the night Jesus had "glory of this nun" was the Feast of the Immaculate Conception. As Christ, the Word, was conceived and brought forth by the immaculately conceived Virgin Mary, so Christ, the Word, was "conceived" and brought forth by the nun in her agony. Again Hopkins has brought together in one resonant image both his theological and his poetic concerns. The creative Word is at the same time the traditional name of God, the God "by whom all things were made," and He is "conceived," is born, in the heart and mind of a human being. It is important to see that the Word is not "reflected" or "mirrored" in the nun. Instead, she cooperates in a mystical marriage to give birth

116

to the Word. The Incarnation is not only a dogma about Jesus of Nazareth, but it is a miracle applicable to all men. God is not only above but is immanent in human beings. In epistemological and aesthetic terms, the Word is not a static reflection of a predetermined external "given" but is a dynamic mode of knowing. Ultimate reality is in some sense created by the verbal articulation of the poem; the functions of priest and poet are joined. This conjunction is the artistic crisis of the poem as it was also a turning point in Hopkins' life.

Stanza 29 praises the nun for her perserverance and her cooperation with God and continues the intricate and meaningful puns on "word."

> Ah! There was a heart right!
> There was single eye!
> Read the unshapeable shock night
> And knew the who and the why;
> Wording it how but by him that present and past,
> Heaven and earth are word of, worded by?—
> The Simon Peter of a Soul! to the blast
> Tarpeïan-fast, but a blown beacon of light.

"The Simon Peter of a soul," fast to the Tarpeian rock, no doubt carried an allusion to Peter's faithfulness and Christ's response in Matthew 16 : 18: "Thou art Peter, and upon this rock I will build my church." Another incident recounted in Matthew's Gospel is even closer to the nun's surrender of her life to the sea. When the disciples' ship was in "the midst of the sea, tossed with waves," by a "contrary" wind, Jesus came to them, "walking on the sea." When Jesus had calmed their first fears, Peter said, "Lord, if it be thou, bid me come to thee on the water. And he said, come. And when Peter was come down out of the ship, he walked on the water to go to Jesus. But when he saw the wind boisterous, he was afraid; and beginning to sink, he cried Lord, save me. And immediately Jesus stretched forth his hand and caught him. . . ." (Matthew 14 : 24–31). Another parallel is Peter's plunging into the sea to meet the risen Christ in John 21 : 7.

The nun, then, who is brought to her death by the external power of God, surrenders to the inner prompting of the Holy Ghost to be a bell of warning to the other poor sheep, the "Comfortless unconfessed of them" who were dying on the *Deutschland.*

> . . . lovely-felicitous Providence
> Finger of a tender of, O of a feathery delicacy, the breast
>   of the
>   Maiden could obey so, be a bell to, ring of it, and
> Startle the poor sheep back! is the shipwrack then a harvest,
>   does tempest carry the grain for thee?

The surrender of the nun to Christ and Hopkins' exploration of its particular significance occur in Stanzas 24–31. The last four stanzas of the poem, 32–35, close the poem with a cosmic universalizing of Hopkins' theme, offered in the form of a prayer of adoration. Both the theme of God's mastery and mercy and the related theme of His outer and inner relation to man are summed up in a series of majestic archetypal sea metaphors.

> I admire thee, master of the tides.
> Of the Yore-flood, of the year's fall;
> The recurb and the recovery of the gulf's sides,
>   The girth of it and the wharf of it and the wall;
> Stanching, quenching ocean of a motionable mind;
> Ground of being, and granite of it: past all
>   Grasp God, throned behind
> Death with a sovereignty that heeds but hides, bodes but
>   abides.

As John Keating has noted, three scriptural treatments of the sea have possibly contributed to the first four lines of this stanza: God's moving over the waters in the creation; the deluge; and God's control of the deeps of the sea in the Book of Job.[9] This stanza also completes

9. Keating, *Deutschland*, 102.

the metaphysical and psychological identification of God with both sea and shore, which was begun in the first stanza. God is not only the "stanching, quenching ocean" of the "motionable mind" of man; He is also "The recurb and the recovery of the gulf's sides, / The girth of it and the wharf of it and the wall." Although the nuns must be drowned in His deeps, He is the "Ground of being, and granite of it." While man is viewed as running sand and water in a well, God is seen as the ultimate forms of these two materials, solid granite and the ocean from which all water comes.[10]

In Stanza 33 God abides

> With a mercy that outrides
> The all of water, an ark
> For the listener; for the lingerer with a love glides
> Lower than death and the dark;
> A vein for the visiting of the past-prayer, pent in prison,
> The-last-breath penitent spirits—the uttermost mark
> Our passion-plungèd giant risen,
> The Christ of the Father compassionate, fetched in the storm
> of his strides.

As the ark was a place of safety in the "Yore-flood" of the old Testament, now Christ is salvation "for the listener" on the stormy sea. I take the last three lines of the stanza to be an independent clause, with "uttermost"—which refers to "The last-breath penitent spirits"—as the subject and "mark" as the verb.[11] The one "fetch" in the nun has fetched "The Christ of the Father compassionate." Christ's "striding" across the water to the penitents recalls His walking on the water to Peter and His symbolic reception into the disciples' ship of John 6 : 18–21: "And the sea arose by reason of a great wind that blew. So when they had rowed about five and twenty or thirty furlongs, they saw Jesus walking on the sea, and drawing

10. Keating, *Deutschland,* 101.
11. See Elisabeth Schneider, "Hopkins' *The Wreck of the Deutschland,* Stanza 33," *Expl.,* 16 (1958), Item 46.

nigh unto the ship: and they were afraid. But he saith unto them, It is I; be not afraid. Then they willingly received him into the ship: and immediately the ship was at the land whither they went."

Stanza 34 continues the archetypal water symbolism for God's coming into the world:

> Not a dooms-day dazzle in his coming nor dark as he came;
> Kind, but royally reclaiming his own;
> A released shower, let flash to the shire, not a lighting of fire hard-hurled.

Not only does God come as the "living water" of John's Gospel, or as the Holy Ghost descending to the Virgin, but there is also a hint of the mythic pattern of Zeus descending to Danae in a golden shower or the rains of the Sky Father impregnating the earth. In the traditional paradox of the Gospel, God is the Father, the lover, and the child of the nun. In the mystic marriage of God and man, He is "new born" from her as He becomes her spouse and her King.

The water imagery, with its filling, brimming, flushing, gushing, stanching, and quenching among the sands of human life, is at last completed in the stark, powerful language of the final stanza:

> Dame, at our door
> Drowned, and among our shoals,
> Remember us in the roads, the heaven-haven of the reward.

The nun's "heaven–haven" of the early poem is to be won only by braving the danger of the sea. Passive withdrawal is not enough. She must surrender, but her surrender must involve active cooperation, as evidenced in the elaborate symbols of a divine marriage. The drowning of the tall nun "at our door" and "among our shoals" leads to the final prayer for the return of the King to England, for the transformation of the nun to be similarly consummated in "English souls," for the indwelling Holy Ghost to be *our* hearts' fire.

Let him easter in us, be a dayspring to the dimness of us,
    be a crimson-cresseted east,
More brightening her, rare-dear Britain, as his reign rolls,
    Pride, rose, prince, hero of us, high-priest,
Our hearts' charity's hearth's fire, our thoughts' chivalry's
    throng's Lord.

John Keble, another Victorian poet–priest, wrote that "Poetry . . . lends Religion her wealth of symbols and similes: Religion restores these again to poetry–clothed with so splendid a radiance that they appear to be no longer merely symbols, but to partake . . . of the nature of sacraments."[12] The term *sacrament* (an outward and visible sign of inward and spiritual grace) best describes the paradox of the transcendent and immanent God, the fearful immensities of the great Other, who in Hopkins' poem becomes *"Our* hearts' charity's hearth's fire." It is the sacramental vision of the universe in "The Wreck of the Deutschland" that allowed Hopkins to resolve the personal and artistic conflict expressed in his early poems. The unfulfilled eroticism of the mermaids is transformed now into the divine love of Christ for the nun, who "bathes" in His "fall-gold mercies," as the ocean in the early poem "drench'd / The floating blooms" and "quench'd / The rosy isles." Unlike the hesitant girl in "The Nix" or the isolated nun of "Heaven–Haven," the nun of "The Wreck" entrusts herself to the sea, and in her total self-giving accepts God's transformation to find her true identity.

    For the moment then, the problem was solved. God was not only above, but was to be found in the midst of human life. The nun's uttering of the word, as indeed Hopkins' own uttering of the poem, had become a dynamic means of knowing God. The symbol of the sea was for Hopkins a means not simply to justify his dual function as priest and poet, but to show their necessary unity.

12. John Keble, *Lectures on Poetry*, trans. E. K. Francis (1912), II, Lecture XL, quoted in W. H. Gardner, *Gerard Manley Hopkins: A Study of Poetic Idiosyncrasy in Relation to Poetic Tradition* (London, Oxford University Press, 1961), II, 238.

In 1882, toward the end of his productive middle period—the years of the sacramental nature poems—Hopkins summed up the theological and poetic doctrine he had articulated with so much difficulty in "The Wreck of the Deutschland," written six years before. "God's utterance of himself in himself is God the Word, outside himself in this world. This world then is word, expression, news of God. Therefore its end, its purpose, its purport, its meaning, is God and its life or work to name and praise him. Therefore praise put before reverence and service."[13] Since the physical world is God's word, His expression, the function of man is to "name and praise" God in the world. This naming and praising is more important than passive reverence or service. Hopkins had apparently burst out of the passive isolation so poignantly chronicled in his early work. He now saw the purpose of man not so much as revering and accepting the given, but as cooperating with God's expression in nature by his own creative expression of the world.

Although Hopkins' attitude at this time may in truth represent a profoundly Christian world view (as I think it does), we must not confuse it with the Roman Catholic or Anglican orthodoxy of his time. As John Henry Newman, Hopkins' spiritual adviser, made clear, Christian doctrine is not a static monolith but an ever-developing organism. Many good critics have distorted our view of Hopkins' work and life by assuming that he can be assimilated to some definable abstract doctrinal position that equals "Roman Catholicism" or "Christian orthodoxy." Yvor Winters, for instance, compared Hopkins unfavorably to Donne because Donne's work presents precise orthodox definitions of human predicaments pow-

13. From *The Sermons and Devotional Writings of Gerard Manley Hopkins*, Christopher Devlin, S.J., ed. (London, published by the Oxford University Press by arrangement with the Society of Jesus, 1959), 129. Hereafter cited as *S.*

erfully and reasonably while Hopkins' presents only emotion, "the illusion of meaning." Donne has "generative concepts," like Original Sin or Grace, while Hopkins has not.[14] But this kind of criticism begs the question: What exactly are the doctrines of Original Sin or Grace? Have they been the same in all ages? Have these concepts been identical in the minds of, say, Jesus, Saint Paul, Thomas Aquinas, Duns Scotus, Martin Luther, Donne, Hans Kung, and Cardinal Spellman?

The work of a friendlier critic than Winters will serve as example. Marshall McLuhan remarked in his intelligent essay, "The Analogical Mirrors," that "Hopkins looks at external nature as a Scripture exactly as Philo Judaeus, St. Paul and the Church Fathers had done." Surely it is obvious that he did not. Hopkins was a modern man. Both Locke and Kant have intervened, not to speak of the elaborate edifice of Thomistic theology. There may be an analogical relationship between Hopkins' and Saint Paul's epistemology, but it is enormously misleading to say that they are identical. We must, if we are to understand aright, consider Hopkins as an innovator, not only in poetry, but in the development of Christian thought as well. In this regard, I would contend that McLuhan's critical terminology betrays a conceptual frame that distorts Hopkins' views as much as it reveals them. The word *mirrors* in his title implies a theory of art and a theology that I believe Hopkins was in the process of abandoning. In his discussion of "The Windhover" McLuhan wrote, "As Hopkins transfers his gaze from the first mirror to the second, we see that his own heart is also a hidden mirror (moral obedience) which flashes to God the image not of 'brute beauty and valour and act' but a 'fire' which is 'a billion times told lovelier'—the chevalier image of Christ."[15] The metaphor of the mirror is taken from an older art theory and a theology different from that of Hopkins and is not entirely applicable to the poem. A

14. *Collection of Critical Essays*, 38–42.
15. *Collection of Critical Essays*, 82–84.

stirring heart and a kindling fire are not mechanical reflections. They cooperate with external forces but are active
and creative (or destructive). Hopkins was, as McLuhan
said, an analogist, but a creative one, not a cool manipula-
tor. The symbols of "The Windhover" express not only
the romantic theory of knowledge and art so perceptively
described by Meyer Abrams, but they also imply a theology considerably different from the deistic externalism
common in his time and somewhat different from the
sort of "imitation" advocated by Saint Ignatius Loyola in
the *Spiritual Exercises*.

Another example of this kind of distortion by
friendly critics is found in the work of Father Robert
Boyle, S.J. Father Boyle's book, *Metaphor in Hopkins*, is
undoubtedly one of the best treatments of Hopkins' poetry. It is precisely the depth of Boyle's critical insight
that, to my mind, makes its distortion more serious—and
ironic. On the surface Boyle seems to recognize the antideist thrust of Hopkins' art. The thesis of his book is
that "Hopkins' nature poems express almost without exception, some facet of divine life in human beings. His
vision of reality focused most clearly on the operation of
Christ's life stemming from the center of the Trinity,
divinizing the hearts of acquiescent humans, reaching
even to animals, birds, trees, the good earth itself."[16]

Boyle's description of metaphor offers a good description of Hopkins' creative epistemology: "This living
process [metaphor] cannot begin without the insemina-
tion of reality, the dynamic union between reality and the
knowing mind." Yet sometimes, unfortunately, not only
do the faithless fable and miss, but even the faithful
waver. It is in the very quality of faithfulness to Catholic
dogma, which is here understood as a clearly definable
and unchanging structure of intellectual propositions,
that Boyle's interpretation of Hopkins is subtly misleading. For instance, there is Boyle's insistence that we must

16. *Metaphor in Hopkins* (Chapel Hill, University of North
Carolina Press, 1960), xi.

accept the words of Hopkins in the Catholic sense in which he intended them. "The reader who has learned his language in a Protestant or in a pagan culture will almost certainly miss the aura of meaning which Hopkins draws from the word 'glory' " [in "The Blessed Virgin Compared to the Air We Breathe"] (p. 51). Certainly the intentions of an author are important, but it is difficult to assert what the "Catholic sense" of words might be. The implication behind Boyle's remarks is the bane of so much otherwise first-class criticism of Hopkins: that only a Jesuit can thoroughly understand his poetry. Now, it is undoubtedly true that a Jesuit can understand certain aspects of it better than a non-Jesuit, but I would assert that in some cases the Jesuit tradition is an obstacle rather than an interpretive guide. If we are to rule out all readers who have learned their language in a "Protestant culture," what are we to do with Hopkins himself, who learned his language in a Protestant culture, who spent most of his life in its midst, and whose two close literary friends were Protestants?

"The most unfortunate tendency among Hopkins' critics," according to Boyle, "in regard to his world–view is that many of them tend to furnish him with one drawn not from the text of his poems or other writings, but from what they think a Catholic world–view is." This is true, but I should like to apply it not only to non-Roman Catholic critics, but to Catholic as well. Following a short discussion of Dante and medieval Christianity, Boyle's statement continues: "Catholics hold precisely the same beliefs that they did then, and a Catholic of the twentieth century who hears or reads *The Divine Comedy* will find himself accepting its ultimate attitudes toward reality with precisely the same sincerity that characterized its acceptance by a comparable Catholic in the fourteenth century. The Catholic tradition has not disintegrated" (p. 192). Certainly, the Catholic tradition has not disintegrated, but it has grown and changed, as the results of Vatican II have made obvious. Tradition is not an abstract system of propositions; it is an organism always in the process of transformation. The idea that "Catholics hold precisely the same beliefs" that they did in the Middle Ages (or in the nineteenth century) is manifest folly. Their ultimate attitudes toward reality may be similar and they may hold these attitudes with sincerity; but that is not the same thing. Father Boyle's mode of thought in this instance, common among Catholics and non-Catholics alike, seems to me to exemplify the rigid patterns of thought we have been discussing. To assert that Catholicism is a fixed, static system, identical in every age, is to distort our perception of Christianity and especially to distort our understanding of Hopkins as a Christian poet. As Cardinal Newman liked to say, "The only sign of life is growth."

It may seem that I am devoting an inordinate amount of space to attack a good critic. I do so because I believe the point is crucial. It is because Boyle's criticism is so generally perceptive that I feel his mode of presenting Hopkins is dangerous. He would doubtless reply that he agrees with me that Hopkins is antideist, that his art is sacramental, that the center of Hopkins' work is the Incarnation—these points make up the theme of his book. What I feel is misleading is the insistence of Boyle and others like him that Hopkins' views were exactly synonymous with Catholic orthodoxy, which, they say, has remained unaltered through the centuries. It is absolutely necessary, if we are to understand Hopkins, to know that his theological views were not identical with the received orthodoxy of his day. It is important for us to know that the terms Father Boyle regards as being received in an identical way by all Catholics—Grace, Incarnation, the Sacred Heart, Mary Immaculate—have not been in the past and are not now always received by all members of the church in the same sense. This is not to say that Hopkins was a cryptopagan, tortured by a repressive Christian belief; it is to say that he was an imaginative Christian poet, working to create and transform that belief.

What then can we say about Hopkins' theory of

poetry and his theological insights during the middle period of his career that has not already been said? J. Hillis Miller, in his treatment of Hopkins in *The Disappearance of God*, suggested that Hopkins had really three theories of poetry, which were ultimately reconciled by his reading of Parmenides.[17] One theory, as expressed in his lecture notes of 1873–1874, is that

> Poetry is speech framed for contemplation of the mind by the way of hearing or speech framed to be heard for its own sake and interest even over and above its interest of meaning. Some matter and meaning is essential to it but only as an element necessary to support and employ the shape which is contemplated for its own sake. . . . Poetry is in fact speech only employed to carry the inscape of speech for the inscape's sake—and therefore the inscape must be dwelt on. (*J*, 289)

This external and manipulative theory must be contrasted, as Miller has pointed out, to Hopkins' interest in a particular kind of diction: "The words which most attract him are those which are a kinesthetic imitation of their meaning, and give a deep bodily, muscular, or visceral possession of the world. For him language originates in a kind of inner pantomime, in fundamental movements of the body and the mind by which we take possession of the world through imitating it in ourselves. Words are the dynamic internalization of the world" (p. 285). Hopkins' vision of a unified harmonious universe therefore led Hopkins to another definition of poetry, according to Miller. "Poetry is not the inscapes of words for the inscape's sake, but an attempt to catch in words the inscapes of things and their interrelation. The business of poetry is the 'representing [of] real things' (*J*, 126), and the tense rhythm of Hopkins' poetry is not so much an attempt to make poetry musical as it is an attempt to echo

17. *The Disappearance of God: Five Nineteenth-Century Writers* (Cambridge, Mass., The Belknap Press of Harvard University Press), 1965.

in words the rhythm of instress as it sweeps through the cosmos, creating inscapes everywhere" (p. 298).

Neither of these two apparently opposed theories was closely related to the problem of self, the isolated selftaste that so concerned Hopkins. The first theory expressed an attitude approaching art for art's sake, a position similar to that of Poe or of Hopkins' tutor Pater. The second theory was more original, but was not completely unlike the imitation theories of the eighteenth century, with their emphasis on representation. These two theories were modified by a third theory, which Hopkins articulated in his spiritual notes: "But MEN OF GENIUS ARE SAID TO CREATE, a painting, a poem, a tale, a tune, a policy; not indeed the colours and the canvas, not the words or notes, but the design, the character, the air, the plan. How then?—from themselves, from their own minds" (S, 238). In the three theories, words, things, and the self are emphasized successively, but the three positions are not joined in one comprehensive aesthetic.

Miller feels that the three separate theories of poetry were reconciled by Hopkins' study of Parmenides. "Nature, language, and thought are seen by Parmenides as the same in being, and this concept of being suggests to Hopkins a way in which he can unify the realms which seem destined to remain disparate. . . . In the Parmenidean fragments Hopkins as early as 1868 finds a way to unify self, words, and world" (pp. 310–11). Miller's discussion goes on to assimilate Parmenides to Hopkins' theology and theory of poetry to outline an all-encompassing system. "Ultimately, with the help of Scotus and other theologians, Hopkins broadens his theory of the Incarnation until he comes to see all things as created in Christ. This doctrine of Christ is a Catholic version of the Parmenidean theory of being, and it is the means by which Hopkins can at last unify nature, words, and selfhood" (pp. 312, 313). Thus Miller's view is that, for Hopkins, poetry ceases to be the place where we confront the "unbridgeable gulfs between world, words, and self."

It becomes the "medium through which man may best express the harmonious chiming of all three in Christ" (p. 317).

I expect that something very much like this was true of Hopkins' attitude toward poetry at the beginning of his middle period. Miller's analysis is certainly consonant with my own interpretation of the significance of "The Wreck of the Deutschland." Although we (as Hopkins himself did) will have to re-examine the idea that the doctrine of Christ is a "Catholic version of the Parmenidean theory of being," Miller's interpretation will serve as a speculative introduction to the conflict Hopkins seems to have resolved at the outset of his mature career.

It is important, however, to look more closely at the results of Hopkins' theorizing, as they are embodied in his poetry of the 1870s. Hopkins' new-found creative theory of poetry (and related theology) may be articulated in four major propositions, which correspond to some of his best-known poems.

The first proposition is that God is immanent; the deists are wrong. Certainly the classic exposition of this theology is found in "God's Grandeur." In this hymn to the Holy Ghost, the Lord and Giver of Life, who spoke in the hearts of the prophets and who conceived Christ in the womb of a human being, Hopkins described a physical world sustained and animated by the power of God within it. Although fire and oil are traditional symbols of the Third Person of the Trinity, Hopkins did not use them in their traditional allegorical sense. Instead, he transformed the two images into natural symbols as they are found within nature, rather than above it—activating principles beneath the surface that give life and meaning to the world.

> The world is charged with the grandeur of God.
>   It will flame out, like shining from shook foil;
>   It gathers to a greatness, like the ooze of oil
> Crushed.

Although electricity and oil are, like God, to be found within the world, Hopkins' poem is not pantheist. God is also transcendent. As in the crisis of the nun in "The Wreck of the Deutschland," the economy of the universe is like a mystic marriage; it implies cooperation between God and the world and between God and man. It is God's metal rod in the Leyden jar of the world that makes its gold foil vibrate. And sometimes, especially in rebellious man, the rod seems to evoke no response.

> Why do men then now not reck his rod?
> Generations have trod, have trod, have trod;
>> And all is seared with trade; bleared, smeared with toil;
>> And wears man's smudge and shares man's smell: the
>> soil
> Is bare now, nor can foot feel, being shod.

Despite man's often observed failure to cooperate with divine forces, Hopkins' poem asserts the continuing presence of inexhaustible reserves of power within nature and the inevitable redemption, which transcends it in the symbol of the Holy Ghost, immanent in His aspect of warm brooder and capable of transcendence with His bright wings in the springing morning.

> And for all this, nature is never spent;
>> There lives the dearest freshness deep down things;
> And though the last lights off the black West went
>> Oh, morning, at the brown brink eastward, springs—
> Because the Holy Ghost over the bent
>> World broods with warm breast and with ah! bright
>> wings.

God, in this poem, is not the celestial watchmaker of the deists, nor is He the Remote Old Man on the sapphire throne, nor the equally remote and dehumanized version of the Son, so often assumed by nineteenth-century orthodoxy. He is, as Hopkins said in "The Wreck" and as Paul Tillich later repeated, "the Ground of Being."

The second proposition implicit in Hopkins' theories of the major period is a corollary of the first. It is that man's physical body is important and inherently valuable; the Manichaeans are wrong. Although critics have traditionally remarked Hopkins' glorification of the body in poems like "Felix Randal" or the Whitmanesque "Harry Ploughman," the more consciously controlled theological treatment of "The Caged Skylark" may serve our purposes better. This poem, written at St. Beuno's in 1877, uses a conceit for the body–spirit dichotomy that is almost trite, a skylark imprisoned in a cage. What Hopkins did with it is not so trite.

> As a dare-gale skylark scanted in a dull cage
>> Man's mounting spirit in his bone-house, mean house, dwells—
> That bird beyond the remembering his free fells;
> This in drudgery, day-labouring-out life's age.

The skylark, confined to his cage, has forgotten his freedom of the open meadows; man's spirit, confined to his cage of bones and flesh, is forced to labor "in drudgery" within the limits of time and space. Both are capable of moments of happiness, moments of beautiful song, but both sometimes rebel against their imprisonment.

> Though aloft on turf or perch or poor low stage,
>> Both sing sometimes the sweetest, sweetest spells,
>> Yet both droop deadly sómetimes in their cells
> Or wring their barriers in bursts of fear or rage.

The sestet attempts the reconciliation of body and soul, finitude and freedom. The answer is not to abandon the body, to give up all limitations for pure spiritual freedom, as the angelic imagination of Poe would have it. The skylark cannot be always flying, but must have his own place.

> Not that the sweet-fowl, song-fowl, needs no rest—
> Why, hear him, hear him babble and drop down to his nest,
>> But his own nest, wild nest, no prison.

131

The conflict between body and spirit is not to be solved by separation, but by transformation. As the bird needs "his own nest," not a prison, so

> Man's spirit will be flesh-bound when found at best,
> But uncumberèd: meadow-down is not distressed
>   For a rainbow footing it nor he for his bónes risen.

The final three lines of the poem assert a traditional Christian doctrine, "the resurrection of the body," and assert it in its most anti-Manichaean sense. Man's spirit assumes its "best" value and meaning only when it is bound by flesh, an "uncumbered" and transformed body. The body is to mark off and order the spirit of man as the rainbow is to "foot" a "meadow-down," to seem to rest on the ground, but to make no physical impact on it. The poem is another expression of the doctrine of the Incarnation, yet this reformulation of a Christian doctrine is quite different in tone from the orthodoxy of its time. There is nothing quite like it in the nineteenth century; there is nothing quite like it in Saint Ignatius Loyola.

I recognize how odd all of this sounds. Nineteenth-century Christians did not, after all, deny the Incarnation or the resurrection of the body. *The Spiritual Exercises* are best known for their imaginative meditational techniques, and the Society of Jesus itself has always been characterized by its involvement with the "world." Nevertheless, accepting a doctrine as an intellectual proposition does not necessarily guarantee sympathy with its spirit. It seems clear enough that Victorian orthodoxy, both Protestant and Catholic, was not in sympathy with the fleshly, physical emphasis of Christianity. Orthodoxy subscribed to the intellectual proposition of the Incarnation of Jesus; Hopkins imaginatively *realized* not only the Incarnation of Jesus, but its corollary, the sanctification of all flesh, the glorification of the body. It is not surprising that he confessed to Bridges that his mind was more like Walt Whitman's than that of any man living. It is also an indication of the conventional attitudes of nineteenth-century orthodoxy toward the body that this should have been an unhappy confession.

132

The first two propositions we have discussed are theological: (1) God is immanent in the world: He is the great Insider; (2) the body is a necessary complement to the spirit: freedom and the divine life are reached through the finite and physical.

The third proposition implicit in Hopkins' middle period is directly related to art: poetry is both creative and cognitive; the mirror aesthetic is wrong. This thesis about poetry we recognized as the foundation and informing principle of "The Wreck of the Deutschland." As the nun uttered the Word, bringing Him into the world, so Hopkins uttered the Word, creating and articulating reality. When he finished the process of the poem, he *knew* more than when he started. "The Wreck" is not simply a reflection of existing Catholic dogma, ornamented by Hopkins' verbal eccentricities; it is a dynamic probing, experiencing, and knowing of some portion of reality. "But MEN OF GENIUS ARE SAID TO CREATE . . . from themselves, from their own minds." Although "The Wreck of the Deutschland" is Hopkins' most ambitious and most detailed exposition of poetry as knowledge, the theme is implicit everywhere, from the ecstatic naming of "Pied Beauty" to the sensuous grasping of God's presence in nature in "Hurrahing in Harvest," in which a cooperative recognition between God and man exists as "the heart hurls for him."

Hopkins used two critical terms of his own coinage to describe the basis for his concept of the creative imagination. They are *inscape,* the inner pattern and distinctive form of natural objects, and *instress,* both the unifying force in the object and the ability in the observer to perceive it, the quality of illumination that allows the observer to know the distinctive pattern that characterizes the object. Thus, on observing grass that looked like hair in December of 1872, Hopkins wrote, "I saw the inscape though freshly, as if my eye were still growing, though with a companion the eye and ear are for the most part shut and instress cannot come" (*J,* 228). Like Ernst Cassirer or Susanne Langer, Hopkins insisted that significant knowledge is found in the pattern or design that transcends while at the same time it includes both subject and object. There is surely a relation between Hopkins' emphasis on the *design* of inscape and the *schema* that Cassirer posited as the object of knowledge. This object cannot be known without the dynamic cooperation of the observer.

> Since, tho' he is under the world's splendour and wonder,
> His mystery must be instressed, stressed;
> For I greet him the days I meet him, and bless when I understand.

The fourth proposition that underlay Hopkins' middle period united his theology and his aesthetics. It includes the other propositions and makes a generative marriage between Hopkins' priestly and poetic vocations. It may be stated simply in a single sentence: The creative imagination of man is the expression of Christ and His continual new birth in the world. Although this proposition, like the previous one, is central to "The Wreck of the Deutschland," perhaps its most spectacular and most direct expression is in the sonnet, "As kingfishers catch fire." The octave of the poem is a hymn in praise of all things that express their individuality, their selfhood—each, in contemporary phrase, "doing its own thing." Significantly—when one remembers the bell–nun identification in "The Wreck"—the last of Hopkins' specific examples is a bell that rings out its own distinctive name.

> As kingfishers catch fire, dragonflies draw flame;
> As tumbled over rim in roundy wells
> Stones ring; like each tucked string tells, each hung bell's
> Bow swung finds tongue to fling out broad its name;
> Each mortal thing does one thing and the same:
> Deals out that being indoors each one dwells;
> Selves—goes itself; *myself* it speaks and spells,
> Crying *What I do is me: for that I came.*

There is nothing unusual or unorthodox, to be sure, in proclaiming the distinctive individuality of animals or inanimate natural objects. Both Hopkins and Roman Catholic orthodoxy would agree that in all "mortal things" except man the "affective will" and the "elective will" are the same. A distinctive individuality and self-hood is what they were created for. But Hopkins went further than this in the sestet—he "said more." The "just man" also proclaims his selfhood, his name, and that name is Christ.

> I say more: the just man justices;
>
> > Keeps gráce; thát keeps all his goings graces;
>
> Acts in God's eye what in God's eye he is—
>
> > Chríst. For Christ plays in ten thousand places,
>
> Lovely in limbs, and lovely in eyes not his
>
> > To the Father through the features of men's faces.

It is through man, "acting" the part of Christ, that Christ plays His role before the Father. It is more than play-acting, Hopkins insisted: the just man *is* Christ in the eyes of God. Christ is born to the world, made *real* in the world by the human imagination. This idea is found, not in the poems alone, but also in Hopkins' spiritual writings, close to the end of his middle period. "It is," he wrote, "as if a man said: That is Christ playing at me and me playing at Christ, only that it is no play but truth; that is Christ being me and me being Christ" (*S*, 154).

It is important to see that Hopkins was not talking of the *Imitatio Christi* in the simple sense of copying or reflecting Christ, as in a mirror. In "The Windhover," for instance, the imitation of Christ is more an imaginative emulation, a reciprocal imitation of creative function than it is a mere reflection of His "mastery." The exciting activity of the bird evokes a complementary response from within the observer. "My heart in hiding / Stirred for a bird,—the achieve of, the mastery of the thing!" When the qualities of the bird are "buckled" to the stirring heart of man, Christ is once more born to the world. "AND the fire that breaks from thee then, a billion

/ Times told lovelier, more dangerous, O my chevalier!"
The reciprocal action of man and Christ, the continual
new birth of Christ in the world through man, is imaged
in the two analogies of the last three lines of the poem.

> No wonder of it: shéer plód makes plough down sillion
> Shine, and blue-bleak embers, ah my dear,
> Fall, gall themselves, and gash gold-vermilion.[18]

These four propositions then—the immanence of
God, the value of the body, poetry as a creative mode
of knowing, and the human imagination as the bearer of
Christ in the world—are fundamental to understanding
Hopkins' most characteristic attitudes toward theology
and poetry during his middle period, roughly the years
1875 to 1882. Judging from the evidence of his poetry,
one might consider these years as an interim of reconciliation. The frightening conflicts of earlier years seem to
have been transcended—at the cost of considerable suffering but with the benefit of increased depth of personality and a new creativity. Despite the apparent solution to
his problems and despite the depth and beauty of that
solution, Hopkins was to write in the succeeding years
poems depicting the most overwhelming personal suffering in all of English literature. The problems of his youth
returned in such terrifying intensity that his best-known
poems of the last years were "written in blood." Our next
task is to find out why this resurgence of once-resolved
conflicts. This will not be easy; the answers we come to
may not fit our preconceptions about Hopkins, about
Christian theology, or about poetry.

THE SEARCH FOR AN INFINITE OBJECT

Although the years 1875–1882 seem to have
brought for Hopkins what amounts to a transformation

18. I am aware of the many other interpretations of the word
buckle and of the sestet in general. I am not concerned to
question other interpretations, which are for the most part
complementary to the one I suggest.

in his theology and his poetics, opposing habits of thought arose with such power that the remainder of his life was characterized by inner turmoil of crisis proportions. There were many reasons for Hopkins' difficulties: ill health, Anglo-Irish politics, overwork, and the speculative possibilities of neuroticism, latent homosexuality, and a cruelly repressed libido.[19] The first three causes are too well documented to require further discussion; the last three possibilities are supported by no concrete evidence at all. Admitting the many possible causes of Hopkins' unhappiness, I should like to investigate an area that has been little considered—at least in the terms we have been using. I should like to continue viewing Hopkins as an innovative thinker wrestling with an evolving Christian theology and an evolving theory of the imagination. Although such investigation must consider Hopkins' psychological state, it generally will take Hopkins seriously as a conscious intellectual who means what he says, rather than as a Jesuit who means what the Church says, or as a neurotic whose significance lies precisely in the fact that he does *not* mean what he says.

*   *   *   *

The Spiritual Exercises of Saint Ignatius, which Hopkins—like all Jesuits—used as the basis of his Long Retreat and which he studied throughout his life as a religious, are preceded by a preliminary topic for meditation, "The First Principle and Foundation." This prolegomenon states the theme of *The Exercises* and presumably is the central guide to the Jesuit spiritual life, if we are able to judge from Hopkins' frequent reference to it in his spiritual writings. The "Principle" reads as follows:

19. Father Devlin suggests that some of Hopkins' difficulties of 1883 were related to the personality of his provincial, Father Edward Ignatius Purbrick: "Confronted with the perfect neatness of the Provincial's mind, with his massive and smoothly-moving deliberation, a wave of diffidence amounting almost to despair seeped up in Hopkins." (*S.*, 214, 215.)

Man is created to praise, reverence, and serve God our Lord, and by this means to save his soul.

The other things on the face of the earth are created for man to help him in attaining the end for which he is created.

Hence, man is to make use of them in as far as they help him in the attainment of his end, and he must rid himself of them in as far as they prove a hindrance to him.

Therefore, we must make ourselves indifferent to all created things, as far as we are allowed free choice and are not under any prohibition. Consequently, as far as we are concerned, we should not prefer health to sickness, riches to poverty, honor to dishonor, a long life to a short life. The same holds for all other things.

Our one desire and choice should be what is more conducive to the end for which we are created.[20]

It is difficult indeed to reconcile this basic guideline of Saint Ignatius and the propositions we have just seen implicit in Hopkins' nature poems of the 1870s. The single-mindedness of Ignatius' "First Principle" may serve as a symbolic key to Hopkins' distress. Ignatius' Counter-Reformation severity can be seen as a theological prologue or perhaps analogue to nineteenth-century habits of thought and language on the one hand and nineteenth-century orthodoxy on the other. It is ironic that it is in a commentary on the "Principle" that Hopkins described the world as "word, expression, news of God," a world whose "end, its purpose, its purport, its meaning, is God and its life or work to name and praise him." Hopkins' version is most striking in its total change of emphasis from its model. In Hopkins' commentary of

20. *The Spiritual Exercises of St. Ignatius, A New Translation Based on Studies in the Language of the Autograph,* Louis Puhl, S.J., ed. (Westminster, Md., Newman Press, 1951), 12. See David A. Downes, *Gerard Manley Hopkins: A Study of His Ignatian Spirit* (New York, Bookman Associates, 1959), for an informative discussion of Hopkins' relationship to Ignatius, but with conclusions that differ somewhat from my own.

1882 God is immanent in the world, expressing Himself; man, therefore, must respond to the creation by naming and praising. Ignatius, in the "Principle," apparently saw a shadow world, meaningful only as an arena for the actions of a separated God and man. Man is not so much to name and praise as to make himself indifferent to the creation. The creation is not inherently valuable or meaningful; it exists to help man to "save his soul." Nature, in this view, is something for man's will to exploit. "Our one desire and choice should be what is more conducive to the end for which we are created."

We may wish to say that there is more to *The Spiritual Exercises* and the Jesuit religious life than the "Principle" and that the "Principle" itself is capable of broader interpretation, as Hopkins' own commentary of 1882 demonstrates. Nevertheless, when the "Principle," joined to the positivist Victorian *Weltanschauung*, came to bear on an overscrupulous conscience like that of Hopkins, the results could be calamitous. We must avoid the critical mistake of injecting current intellectual predispositions into a poet of an earlier time; Hopkins was very much a man of his age. Although his theological insights of the middle period have much in common with twentieth-century theologians, Hopkins always regarded himself as an orthodox Catholic and, as his early letters show, felt an almost obsessive compulsion to maintain that orthodoxy. No one could be more orthodox than Saint Ignatius, but Victorian Christianity in general interpreted his writings far differently than Hopkins did at the end of his middle period. Conflict was inevitable. Hopkins' increasingly severe and single-minded interpretation of the "Principle" in later years and his 1882 immanentist commentary on it form, symbolically at least, the poles of the intellectual and spiritual struggle that so racked him during the last seven years of his life.

Are God and His creation totally separate, as Victorian orthodoxy and a strict reading of Ignatius' "Principle" might imply? Is the creation simply a neutral stage setting for the naked wills of God and man? Or is the creation "word, expression, news of God"? Is the world's body important or only man's "soul"? Is the human imagination valuable or only the will? Hopkins was torn between his sense of duty toward the will as a Jesuit and a Victorian, and his affinity for nature and the world of imagination as a poet. The problem, of course, had many sources besides Ignatius. The general conflict had been stated by Tennyson in *In Memoriam:* "Are God and Nature then at strife?"

The Ignatian severity is evident in Hopkins' letter to Canon Dixon of 1883, in which he explains his reluctance to publish his poems: "Our Society values, as you say, and has contributed to literature, to culture; but only as a means to an end. Its history and its experience show that literature proper, as poetry, has seldom been found to be to that end a very serviceable means" (*Correspondence,* p. 93).

During the eighties Hopkins apparently swung away from his synthesis of the nature poems and back toward the point of view symbolized by Ignatius' "Principle," the point of view evident in so many of his early poems. He became impaled on the medieval dilemma that presented the "elective will" *(voluntas ut arbitrium)* and the "affective will" *(voluntas ut natura).* He seems to have leaned increasingly toward the theory that human salvation depends solely on the *arbitrium*, on choice rather than desire.[21] On September 5, 1883, he wrote:

> The memory, understanding and affective will are incapable themselves of an infinite object and do not tend towards it; they are finite powers and can get each an adequate object. But the tendency in the soul towards an infinite object comes from the *arbitrium*. The *arbitrium* in itself is man's personality or individuality and places him

21. Hopkins wrote on Sept. 3, 1883, *"Desiderando et eligendo:* here distinction of affective and elective will." (*S,* 130.) See Devlin's intelligent but somewhat different interpretations of these matters (*S,* 115–21); also Miller's similar interpretation, 330.

on a level of individuality in some sense with God. (*S*, 138, 139)

The insistence here on the separation of human faculties from God and the importance of the arbitrary will as the sole link between the soul and an infinite object again betrays a shift in Hopkins' thinking from the immanent-ist theology of his commentary of 1882 on the "Princi-ple" and his poetry of the previous years to a transcendentalist and externalist interpretation of Ig-natius. The phrase, "infinite object," as applied to God, is quite different from the "ground of being, granite of it," of "The Wreck of the Deutschland."

J. Hillis Miller has suggested, as observed earlier, that Hopkins' first attempt at a synthesis of his various theories of poetry, his reconciliation of the self, words, and reality, was made possible by his reading of Parme-nides in 1868. All things became valuable for him as they became unified, in Parmenidean theory, in "being." I would suggest that Hopkins' difficulties of the eighties also have their seed in the Parmenidean philosophy, un-derstood in the abstract atmosphere of Victorian rational-ism, for if all things are valuable in being, all things may similarly be worthless or unreal. This is the classic conun-drum of pantheism. If God is everything, how is one to distinguish between a cancer and the surgeon who kills it? Hopkins seems to have looked through the Parmenidean spyglass by its opposite end and to have been horrified by what he saw. Although the Christian theology of "The Wreck" or "The Windhover" could hardly be called pantheist, Hopkins seems to have developed grave doubts about the theology behind them. Influenced by the sin-gle-minded asceticism of Saint Ignatius and nineteenth-century orthodoxy, he apparently was almost overwhelmed by what William Lynch has called in an-other context the "Parmenidean univocity." The univo-cal mode of thought, Lynch has explained, is always tempted "to reduce everything, like and unlike, to a flat community of sameness—all in the name of an intelligibility and type of order that does not and cannot belong to the real world. Instead of trying to handle the difference or submitting it to other faculties that might discover intelligibility in it, it tends in various ways to eliminate the unlike, the different, the pluralistic, as a kind of intractable and even hostile material."[22] In Parmenides' view of the world there can be neither change nor history. "Nothing new can come to be; for that would mean it once *was not;* it cannot die, for that would mean a passage into a fabulous and impossible non-being. Being is fixed; Fate has fixed it, motionless, altogether everywhere, triumphant." The univocal attitudes to reality, Lynch said further, "are, principally, a leveling of the real, a manipulation of it in the interests of the One, and a foreshortening of the insights that can come only from a richer penetration into the more complicated materials present in actuality itself" (pp. 126, 127).

The univocal mind–set has not been limited to the pre-Socratic philosopher. It bears an interesting analogy, at least, to the externalist epistemology we have been discussing. It has obvious relevance to one's conception of art. When a univocal world view is imposed from above, there is no longer any need for the creative imagination. Since, for the univocal mind, the great chain of being exists already, independent from human observers, its further articulation in art becomes a waste of time and an occasion for the sin of pride—for the demonic, as Hopkins implied in his meditation on hell. Man is not to create, but to obey. Man's duty is not so much cooperation with God as a responsible son, but passive acceptance of the paternal will. The human imagination becomes useless, illusory, or specifically sinful when it is considered in the light of a Parmenidean univocity joined to nineteenth-century orthodoxy and Ignatian asceticism.

Hopkins, then, the once enthusiastic praiser and namer of

22. From *Christ and Apollo* by William F. Lynch, S.J., © 1960 Sheed and Ward, Inc., New York. P. 122.

All things counter, original, spare, strange;
    Whatever is fickle, freckled (who knows how?)
    With swift, slow; sweet, sour; adazzle, dim;

became again obsessed with the vision of a vacant creation animated only by the tortured will of man in its
search for an "infinite object." As Devlin has put it, "He
exaggerated Scotus' distinction between nature and individuality; he assigned all his love of beauty to the *voluntas ut natura* and all his desire for holiness to the naked
arbitrium, instead of remembering that the love of beauty
is—as Scotus says it is—the initial impulse to the love of
God" (*S*, 120). If it is true that human beings can love
only what is presented to them, it follows that, if the
arbitrium rejects the world, it rejects God or at least will
be unable to find Him.

If the central meaning of the world is the *arbitrium*
and its search for God—God understood as an "infinite
object"—poetry becomes, as Hopkins told Bridges, a far
less "serviceable means" to that end. It is not that poetry
is necessarily bad; it is trivial. It is not, as it had seemed
earlier, a means of knowing God. It may even become an
obstacle to knowing Him. Like many other attempts to
know God without intermediary involvement in the natural world and without the creative imagination, Hopkins'
attempt was doomed to failure. The powerful and life-
giving tradition of Christianity and the continuing support of the Roman Catholic Church were of no avail
when Hopkins came to believe, according to a rationalized orthodoxy, that their only significance was to train
his soul to transcend the world itself in choosing God.
"There can be no depth," Paul Tillich wrote, "without
the way to depth. Truth without the way to truth is
dead."[23] Hopkins' meditation on the "Principle" in June
of 1884—"Facere nos indifferentes—with the elective
will, not the affective will essentially; but the affective will

23. *The Shaking of the Foundations* (New York, Charles Scrib-
ner's Sons, 1948), 55.

will follow"—leads thus to a tragic impossibility (S, 256). For a man like Hopkins, natural desire could never be satisfied with a rejection of creation.

Miller has written of Hopkins' retreat notes of 1888 that "There is a strange similarity between the final stance of Hopkins and that of Matthew Arnold" (p. 358). It is perhaps true that Hopkins, like Arnold, developed profound doubts about the validity of the creative imagination and apparently lost his sense of God's immanence as Arnold lost confidence in Marguerite and all she represented. Yet it is also true that Hopkins' most interesting poetry, like Arnold's, was written during the years of most acute personal crisis: "Dover Beach" has analogues in "Carrion Comfort" and "No worst, there is none." More striking is the fact that, despite his professed suspicion of poetry and his sense of guilt at occupying himself with it, Hopkins did not stop creating poems. Like Saint Alphonsus at the door, he fought a "war within," articulating in a series of terrifying poems his maturest expression of the conflict between the affective will and the elective, between an immanent God and a transcendent, between the creative imagination of man and his passive acceptance of the given. He wrestled not only with himself and with his God, but with the central problems of his age.

POETRY: SELF-PRAISE OR SELF-KNOWLEDGE?

Although the course of Hopkins' struggle is reflected in his spiritual writing and in his letters, what must most concern us is the record formed by his later poems, the "terrible sonnets." His conflict is inextricably involved with the question of language. If the creative imagination is irrelevant, if nature is merely a tool to be exploited by the naked will in its striving for spiritual union with God, words become meaningless. They merely reflect a universe that in itself is valueless. Words are inevitably bound to the prison of the self, except in their expression of pure volition toward God. They take a place in a rationalized theological orthodoxy quite similar to the place of poetry in the art for art's sake aesthetics of Poe: truth and poetry are like oil and water.

Hopkins was aware of this emasculation of language as it occurred in some scientific writing. In a letter to Dixon in 1886 about his own proposed essay on "Light and the Ether," he remarked how dependence on formulaic thought in scientific books tended to separate people from nature rather than join them to it in greater understanding.

> The study of physical science has, unless corrected in some way, an effect the very opposite of what one would suppose. One would think it might materialize people (no doubt it does make them or, rather I should say, they become materialists; but that is not the same thing: they do not believe in Matter more but in God less); but in fact they seem to end in conceiving only of a world of formulas, with its being properly speaking in thought, towards which the outer world acts as a sort of feeder, supplying examples for literary purposes. (*Correspondence*, p. 139)

What Hopkins has described here is again very much like Blake's prison of self-hood, Ulro, a state occasioned by Locke's epistemology. What Hopkins did not see so clearly was that the formulas of Victorian orthodoxy and Ignatius' "Principle" did not necessarily "divinize people"; rather, it made them deists. They did not believe in God more (He lived, alas, away), but in man and nature less.

Nevertheless, there is more to the Christian tradition than the deist tendency of the nineteenth century, more to Ignatius and the Jesuit spiritual life than the "Principle," more to Victorian theories of language and art than positivism. Similarly, there is a great deal more to Hopkins' theology and poetics than a stark renunciation of the world. The later sonnets are "terrible," not so much because they reflect a solid commitment to a rationalized orthodoxy, but because they record Hopkins' most agonized formulation of the conflict between two theologies and between two theories of poetry and language. In fact, contrary to his own apparent belief, it is Hopkins' imagination rather than his elective will that saves him. It is in the struggle of the later poems that his antideist theology and antirationalist poetics are rendered valid by an imagination both creative and fully Christian.

*   *   *   *

The poetic prelude to Hopkins' last sonnets of desolation is perhaps the most terrible of all: "Spelt from Sibyl's Leaves." Growing out of his meditations during the Long Retreat of his tertianship of 1881—especially the meditation on hell and the devil—and his succeeding notes of the next three years, the poem was begun in October of 1884 and finished two years later (*P,* xlii). Chronologically, it parallels the black winter of 1884–1885; thematically, it treats the crisis Hopkins attempted to resolve during the remaining years of his life. It was his own mysterious "oracle," uttered in the traditional ambiguity of the Sibyl and framed against approaching nightfall and the gates of hell.[24]

The central inspiration of Hopkins' meditations of 1881, from which "Sibyl's Leaves" ultimately grew, was apparently what he termed "the great sacrifice," which Father Devlin believes he saw "at once as the divine history of the universe and as the private ideal of his own life, his own special insight into the mind and heart of God" (*S,* 107). As Hopkins explained in a letter to Bridges:

> Christ's life and character are such as appeal to all the
> world's admiration, but there is one insight St. Paul gives

24. Paul L. Mariani's *A Commentary on the Complete Poems of Gerard Manley Hopkins* (Ithaca, Cornell University Press, 1970) appeared too late for me to use it extensively. His discussion of "Spelt from Sibyl's Leaves" (197–209) points out the poem's relation to Hopkins' meditation on hell as mine does, although we arrived at our interpretations independently.

us of it which is very secret and seems to me more touching and constraining than everything else is. This mind he says, was in Christ Jesus—he means as man: being in the form of God—that is, finding, as in the first instant of his incarnation he did, his human nature informed by the godhead—he thought it nevertheless no snatching-matter for him to be equal with God, but annihilated himself, taking the form of a servant; that is, he could not but see what he was, God, but he would see it as if he did not see it, and be as if he were not and instead of snatching at once at what all the time was his, or was himself, he emptied or exhausted himself so far as that was possible, of godhead and behaved only as God's slave, as his creature, as man, which also he was, and then being in the guise of man humbled himself to death, the death of the cross. It is this holding of himself back and not snatching at the truest and highest good, the good that was his right, nay his possession from a past eternity in his other nature, his own being and self, which seems to me the root of all his holiness and the imitation of this the root of all moral good in other men.[25]

It was the failure of Lucifer and the rebel angels, Adam and Eve, and all men to join harmoniously in Christ's cosmic sacrifice that brought about sin and hell. Hopkins' related meditation on hell and the fall of Lucifer thus takes on enormous significance when we think of it as an introduction to "Spelt from Sibyl's Leaves" and as a subject that bears direct relevance for the creative artist. In Hopkins' view the refusal of the great sacrifice and the consequent fall from heaven threw all the energy and "instress" of the rebel angels back upon themselves to form an isolating prison. Their individualistic search for light resulted in darkness.

25. From *The Letters of Gerard Manley Hopkins to Robert Bridges*, Claude Colleer Abbott, ed., rev. ed. (London, published by the Oxford University Press by arrangement with the Society of Jesus, 1955), 175.

This throwing back or confinement of their energy is a dreadful constraint or imprisonment and, as intellectual action is spoken of under the figure of light, it will in this case be an imprisonment in darkness, a being in the dark; for darkness is the phenomenon of foiled action in the sense of sight. But this constraint and this blindness or darkness will be most painful when it is the main stress or energy of the whole being that is thus balked.

This main stress, according to Hopkins, is their natural tendency toward God; thus, we have apparently the first fatal disjuncture between the affective and the elective will, a divorce that results in the hellish self-torture of the fallen angels (S, 137, 138). Hopkins continued his description of the angels, likening their situation to Saint Theresa's vision of hell:

> The understanding open wide like an eye, towards truth in God, towards light; is confronted by that scape, that act of its own, which blotted out God and so put blackness in the place of light; does not see God but sees that, so giving a meaning to something I remember in St. Theresa's vision of hell to this effect: "I know not how it is, but in spite of the darkness the eye sees there all that to see is most afflicting." Against these acts of its own the lost spirit dashes itself like a caged bear and is in prison, violently instresses them and burns, stares into them and is the deeper darkened. (S, 138)

Even more significant is Hopkins' idea that the fall of Satan resulted from his pride in helping the angel choir to sing at the creation. Instead of joining Christ's great sacrifice in his proper place, he was seduced by the sound of his own voice.

> This was the process of his own fall. For being required to adore God and enter into a covenant of justice with him he did so indeed, but, as a chorister who learns by use in the church itself the strength and beauty of his voice, he became aware in his very note of adoration of the riches of his nature; then when from that first note he should

148

have gone on with the sacrificial service, prolonging the first note instead and ravished by his own sweetness and dazzled, the prophet says, by his beauty, he was involved in spiritual sloth ("nolendo se adjuvare") and spiritual luxury and vainglory. (S, 179–80)

The strange wording of this description and its unusual metaphor compel one's attention. How odd to describe Satan as a "chorister" who learned his art in the "church itself," and then was distracted from his duty in the sacrificial service by the dazzling beauty of his own singing. It is possible, even likely, that Hopkins was drawing with a frightened shudder a parallel to his own artistic career. Did not he himself learn an art of surpassing beauty and originality as God's chorister in the Society of Jesus? And when he had sounded that first note (the nature poems?), was he not tempted to prolong it at the cost of his soul?

This song of Lucifer's was a dwelling on his own beauty, an instressing of his own inscape, and like a performance on the organ and instrument of his own being; it was a sounding, as they say, of his own trumpet and a hymn in his own praise. Moreover it became an incantation: others were drawn in; it became a concert of voices, a concerting of selfpraise, an enchantment, a magic, by which they were dizzied, dazzled, and bewitched. (S, 200–201)

The example of Lucifer brings Hopkins' chastened theology to bear on art and the value of the creative imagination. Lucifer's art, like Poe's, was only self-expressive; like the angelic song of Israfel, it was unrelated to external reality. It was an incantation "dwelling on his own beauty," and therefore, for Hopkins, it was devilish. Although Hopkins nowhere made a specific application of his ideas on the fall from heaven to his theory of poetry as such, the evidence of both his life and his writing leaves the impression that always at the back of his mind after the retreat of 1881 was the warning and prophetic vision of Satan as the archetypal artist, singing blindly in the ever-growing blackness of hell as the divorce between his affective and elective will became total and final.

With this background in mind we can now turn to "Spelt from Sibyl's Leaves." Hopkins had written that "the fall from heaven was for the rebel angels what death is for man" (S, 137). "Spelt from Sibyl's Leaves" is a poem about the approach of night and death and a prophecy of their significance for a Christian who was also a creative artist. The title of the poem brings to mind the words of the *Dies Irae*, when David and the Sibyl foretell the terrors that will confront the soul at judgment. Also pertinent is Aeneas' quest for prophecy at the Sibyl's cave and his descent into hell in the common mythic pattern of the underground journey.

The octave sets the scene of approaching darkness. The coming of evening leads to its symbolic parallel, the imminence of death and judgment. The glories of the created universe are dissolving in the deepening twilight; the dappled world is being "dismembered," to leave only the isolated self in its apparent separation from both nature and God.

> Earnest, earthless, equal, attuneable, | vaulty, voluminous, . . . stupendous
> Evening strains to be tíme's vást, | womb-of-all, home-of-all, hearse-of-all night.
> Her fond yellow hornlight wound to the west, | her wild hollow hoarlight hung to the height
> Waste; her earliest stars earlstars, | stárs principal, over-bend us,
> Fíre-féaturing heaven. For earth | her being has unbound; her dapple is at an end, as-
> tray or aswarm, all throughther, in throngs; | self ín self steepéd and páshed—Quíte
> Disremembering, dísmémbering | áll now. Heart, you round me right
> With: Óur évening is over us; óur night | whélms, whélms, ánd will end us.

150

The dappled loveliness of "Pied Beauty" or the delicate form of the bluebell by which Hopkins knew "the beauty of Our Lord" is no longer relevant. All that remains is "self in self," like the rebel angels, "steeped and pashed."

The relation to hell and Lucifer is made even more apparent by the descriptive lines that open the sestet:

> Only the beakleaved boughs dragonish | damask the tool-
> smooth bleak light; black,
> Ever so black on it.

The adjective "dragonish" was especially significant for Hopkins. Six days before his commentary on Lucifer's song he had written a long series of notes on dragons and their relation to Satan.

> The snake or serpent a symbol of the Devil. So also the Dragon. . . . Now among the vertebrates the reptiles go near to combine the qualities of the other classes in themselves and are, I think, taken by the Evolutionists as nearest the original vertebrate stem and as the point of departure for the rest. In this way clearly dragons are represented as gathering up the attributes of many creatures. . . . And therefore I suppose the dragon as a type of the Devil to express the universality of his powers, both the gifts he has by nature and the attributes and sway he grasps, and the horror which the whole inspires. . . . The dragon then symbolizes one who aiming at every perfection ends by being a monster, a "fright." (*S*, 199)

Hopkins' description here links the dragon closely to his later discussion of Lucifer, the prideful singer, and thence perhaps to the fallen artist. We have in fact a very subtle version of the dragon symbolism of early Tennyson poems like "The Kraken" or "The Hesperides." The relationship becomes even clearer when we consider Hopkins' unfinished poem, No. 150, which Bridges took as a first sketch for "Spelt from Sibyl's Leaves."

> The times are nightfall, look, their light grows less;
> The times are winter, watch, a world undone:

. . . .

Or what is else? There is your world within.
There rid the dragons, root out there the sin.
Your will is law in that small commonweal. . . .

The dragons who inhabit the depths of the self are archetypes of Lucifer, of demonic self-will. Hopkins' "world within" has become a battlefield, a scene of conflict between two "selves": the devilish dragon, associated with art and self-love, versus the ascetic and submissive will of the knight of Ignatius. Freud might have viewed the battle as between id and superego.

The Sibyl's "oracle" is presented in the sestet. It envisions the terrors of ultimate judgment and hell in imagery reminiscent of Virgil, of Matthew's account of Christ dividing the sheep and the goats, and of Hopkins' meditations of 1881 and the years following, on hell and the fallen angels.

> Óur tale, O óur oracle! | Lét life, wáned,
>   ah lét life wind
> Off hér once skéined stained véined variety | upon, áll on
>   twó spools; párt, pen, páck
> Now her áll in twó flocks, twó folds—black, white; | right,
>   wrong; reckon but, reck but, mind
> But thése two; wáre of a wórld where bút these | twó
>   tell, each off the óther; of a rack
> Where, selfwrung, selfstrung, sheathe- and shelterless, |
>   thóughts agaínst thoughts ín groans grínd.

In the end, earth will unbind her being. All is irrelevant but the relation of man's will to God. In the Sibyl's vision, the divorce between the affective and elective wills is complete. One must be either a knight or a dragon; there is no life between. The more powerful the personality involved, the more acute the horror. As Hopkins said of the rebel angels in their darkness, "it follows, geometrically, the greater the aversion the greater the pain and, morally, the greater the disobedience the greater the pain;

The keener the consciousness the greater the pain;
The greater the stress of being the greater the pain;
both these show that the higher the nature the greater
the penalty. (*S*, 138)

In the same meditation of 1883, in which he attributed
man's sole link to God to the *arbitrium*, Hopkins used
terminology that recurs in "Spelt from Sibyl's Leaves"
and indicates the psychological and theological atmosphere from which the poem derives.

> God is good and the stamp, seal, or instress he sets on each
> scape if of *right, good,* or of *bad, wrong.* Now the sinner
> who has preferred his own good, as revenge, drunkenness,
> to God's good, and God, by his attachment to which and
> God's reflection of it he is carried and swept away to an
> infinite distance from God; and the stress and strain of his
> removal is his eternity of punishment. (*S*, 139)

The oracle of Sibyl's cave, then, is in many ways a
theological version of Empedocles' unhappy song on
Mount Etna. God is not immanent in the creation, which
has disappeared. He is not even mentioned in "Sibyl's
Leaves." The creative imagination is an illusion, which
only makes greater pain in a world where nothing but the
will remains, a world where "seeing the object as in itself
it really is" means only the agony of moral choice. Although the language describing a hell to be avoided derives from Hopkins' discussion of the fallen angels, he
prefaced the sestet with the words, "Our tale. O our
oracle!" It is, in fact, impossible to distinguish between
his vision of a world stripped of everything but moral
choice and hell itself. For a priest who defined his orthodoxy in the terms of the meditation on hell but who
aspired to be a creative artist, the tension in the poem is
nearly unbearable. Well might he prophesy for himself

a rack
Where, selfwrung, selfstrung, sheathe- and shelterless, |
thóughts agaínst thoughts ín groans grínd.

153

Before turning to Hopkins' further development in the terrible sonnets, it may be useful to consider an unfinished fragment written at the same time as "Spelt from Sibyl's Leaves," which throws additional light on the significance of the latter poem. I refer to Caradoc's soliloquy from Act II of *St. Winefred's Well,* a play Hopkins began in October of 1879 and worked at, on and off, through subsequent years. The soliloquy has been dated as contemporary with "Sibyl's Leaves" (P, 314). Immediately preceding the soliloquy the Welsh chieftain Caradoc has murdered Winefred, Saint Beuno's niece, by cutting off her head as she defends her chastity. He describes his feelings after this mutilation in a long speech, dwelling on her beauty and his own subsequent isolation. His speech has the majesty of a fallen Lucifer:

> And I do not repent;
> I do not and I will not | repent, not repent.
> The blame bear who aroused me. | What Í have done violent
> I have líke a líon dóne, | líonlíke dóne,
> Honouring an uncontrolled | royal wrathful nature,
> Mantling passion in a grandeur, | crimson grandeur.
> Now be my pride then perfect, | all one piece. Henceforth
> In a wide world of defiance | Caradoc lives alone,
> Loyal to his own soul, laying his | ówn law down, no law nor
> Lord now curb him for ever. | O daring! O deep insight!
> What is virtue? Valour; | only the heart valiant.
> And right? Only resolution; | will, his will unwavering
> Who, like me, knowing his nature | to the heart home, nature's business,
> Despatches with no flinching. | But wíll flesh, O can flésh
> Second this fiery strain? | Not always; O no no!
> We cannot live this life out; | sometimes we must weary
> And in this darksome world | what comfort can I find?
> Down this darksome world | cómfort whére can I find
> When 'ts light I quenched; its rose, | time's one rich rose, my hand,

154

By her bloom, fast by | her fresh, her fleecèd bloom,
Hideous dáshed dówn, leaving | earth a winter withering
With no now, no Gwenvrewi.

In the demonic pride of Caradoc and his dependence on
"will unwavering" we see the hell of the fallen angels and
once more the divorce of the elective and affective wills:
"But will flesh, O can flesh / Second this fiery strain? Not
always; O no no!" Presumably, Caradoc is like Lucifer in
that he has followed a distorted *arbitrium* in opposition
to his affective will. He has cut off "time's one rich rose"
with his own hand. His murder of Winefred has also been
an act of self-mutilation:

I all my being have hacked | in half with hér neck.

Caradoc's soliloquy is complementary to "Sibyl's
Leaves" and clarifies the psychological tension of that
poem. The Sibyl's ambiguous oracle stresses the end of
the created world and the paramount importance of the
elective will, but it is unclear as to whether this analysis
of reality is a reminder of the danger of hell or is hell itself.
In "St. Winefred's Well" Caradoc stifles the affective
will with the elective "will unwavering" in demonic self-
mutilation or, as the Freudians might put it, self-castra-
tion. It is as though Hopkins were trying on alternate
theologies. If Victorian orthodoxy and a strictly literal
interpretation of Ignatius' "Principle" are correct, then
one is well warned to concentrate on the elective will at
no matter what cost to avoid the hell of eternal separation
from God. If the theology of the nature poems is correct,
the total emphasis on will without the creative imagination or nature *is* hell, as is evidenced by one interpretation of "Sibyl's Leaves" and by Caradoc's murder of
Winefred. Ironically, both Caradoc and the rebel angels
fall by rejecting their nature to follow their own individual arbitrary wills.

"Spelt from Sibyl's Leaves" and the fragmentary
soliloquy of Caradoc, growing as they do from the anguish
of the terrible winter of 1884–1885 and from the self-

lacerating spiritual notes of the preceding three years, mark Hopkins' theological, intellectual, and aesthetic conflict at its crisis. The soul-wrenching agony of his youth had returned with a seemingly irreconcilable intensity. The intensity was more acute because of Hopkins' greater development as a poet and more profound self-knowledge. As he had said of the fallen angels:

> The keener the consciousness the greater the pain;
> The greater the stress of being the greater the pain:
> both these show that the higher the nature the greater the penalty.

There is a temptation, always, to search for a catastrophe after a crisis—or for some reasonable denouement —to bring the plot to a satisfying conclusion. In reflecting on the stresses of Hopkins' life, it would be gratifying to say, with many of Hopkins' Catholic apologists that after a difficult period of Christian probation or spiritual dryness he resolved his conflicts, found his God, and died at peace, as evidenced by his reported deathbed utterance: "I'm so happy, so happy." Or, one might prefer the rationally satisfying view of some of Hopkins' secular critics who regard his life as a tragedy. In this interpretation, Hopkins was a natural poet (possibly a cryptopagan) whose flaw was a self-willed sacrifice of himself and his talent to the Society of Jesus and an outmoded Christian belief, as evidenced by the personal catastrophe expressed in the terrible sonnets.

As far as I know, the evidence of the last four years of his life fully supports neither view. Although Hopkins could write the ecstatic "Heraclitean Fire" the year before he died and could tell Bridges that he was in good spirits despite illness, he wrote "helpless loathing" repeatedly in his retreat notes of 1888. His last poem refers to his "winter world." It is equally true, however, that both interpretations of the close of Hopkins' life do have much to recommend them. His late writings have much in common with well-known experiences of Christian probation. Hopkins was not paralyzed by despair; rather, he attempted to overcome it. He was, certainly, held in the grip of an overscrupulous conscience. There is no doubt that he struggled, not necessarily with Christianity, but with a rationalized form of it. The truth does not lie between the two interpretations, as in a compromise, but in a dynamic tension between the two, in the state of conflict itself.

The essence of Hopkins' life and work both first and last—its inscape—was conflict, a conflict he could never satisfactorily resolve. The terrible sonnets, for instance, never reflect a decision, never express, as Winters aptly said, a "generating concept." They are more like a process, a creative, probing attempt through language to know and grasp the real and to reconcile it to the self.

In "I wake and feel the fell of dark" we have an extension of the desolation of "Sibyl's Leaves," this time more personally stated and more directly related to the function of the creative artist. The poem describes hell: the hell of the isolated human self in a deist universe and the hell of the isolated artist for whom the imagination is an illusion and language a useless and empty mechanism. Hopkins' situation in the poem is very much like that of Merlin, bound and helpless in the dark woods of Broce-liande. He wakes to "feel the fell of dark, not day." God, like the God of the deists, "lives alas! away." He is trapped within the prison of the self, his words are "cries like dead letters sent." This state of alienation and darkness corresponds to the dark hell of the fallen angels.

> I see
> The lost are like this, and their scourge to be
> As I am mine, their sweating selves; but worse.

As in "Sibyl's Leaves," the "selfyeast of spirit" brings torture: "my taste was me." Here, Hopkins is unable to resolve his conflict, frankly to side with "the lost" who are like him. He must continue his internal struggle with the last two words of the poem: "I see / The lost are like this . . . but worse."

"No worst, there is none" chronicles a similar desolation, but, ironically, it uses the categories of the creative imagination to overcome it. Its strategy is not to invoke the elective will to overcome a crushing sense of despair but to employ the resources of language to objectify and to understand the experience. Working within the Christian devotional tradition, Hopkins used the imaginative methods of the 22nd Psalm (the 21st, in the Douay version), the Book of Job, and the creative meditational techniques of Saint Ignatius as a means of knowing his own situation. He enriched the experience with the analogies of King Lear, the blind Gloucester, Prometheus, and Jesus Christ. Yvor Winters was right in discerning the lack of a "generating concept" in the poem, a preconceived or pre-existent premise to make into poetry; he was quite wrong in then dismissing the poem as having only the "illusion of meaning." Rather, Hopkins came to know his meaning through the archetypal symbols of unmerited suffering in the psalm, Job, Prometheus, Lear, and Christ. In the octave in which "My cries heave, herds-long," we are reminded of the anguished cry of the psalm: "O God my God . . . why hast thou forsaken me?" a cry repeated by Christ on the cross. The lament of the speaker of the poem, inexplicably heaving over the herds, may refer to verse 13 of this Good Friday psalm: "Many calves have surrounded me: fat bulls have besieged me." The sestet is animated by the symbols of Prometheus or the blind Gloucester suffering on the cliff, Lear in the storm, and Job in God's whirlwind.

> O the mind, mind has mountains; cliffs of fall
> Frightful, sheer, no-man-fathomed. Hold them cheap
> May who ne'er hung there. Nor does long our small
> Durance deal with that steep or deep. Here! creep,
> Wretch, under a comfort serves in a whirlwind: all
> Life death does end and each day dies with sleep.

The significance for Hopkins in the stories of the suffering protagonists alluded to is that all were illuminated by their suffering. All achieved some measure of self-knowledge and knowledge of God. All were enabled to continue their lives in this knowledge, if only to be able to meet death itself, as in the case of Lear or Christ. The Lord, answering Job out of the whirlwind, tells him to "gird up thy loins like a man" (Job, 40: 2). Through a tense but creative juxtaposition of his own state and the mythic imagination of the past, both secular and biblical, Hopkins also was able to come to increased knowledge and peace, although the peace was more like an armed truce: "all / Life death does end and each day dies with sleep." The delicate balance is apparent in the ambiguous syntax: Is "life" the subject of "does end" or is "death"? Is the daily advent of sleep a despairing prophecy of death and endless oblivion, or is it a recurrent release from pain that precedes regeneration? In the depths of desolation, the conflict of despair and imagination results in a creative tension of self-knowledge and beauty.

In "My own heart let me have more pity on" Hopkins clarified the terms of his inner struggle with greater equanimity. The poem does not express a resolution but an attempt, as in No. 68, "Patience," to live with his problem patiently. It was Hopkins' recognition of the futility of setting the elective will in continual opposition to the affective: "let / Me live to my sad self hereafter kind, / Charitable." The process of the terrible sonnets had made him aware that his state was similar to the hell of the fallen angels or Caradoc's search for comfort in "this darksome world."

> I cast for comfort I can no more get
> By groping round my comfortless, than blind
> Eyes in their dark can day or thirst can find
> Thirst's all-in-all in all a world of wet.

But God is not commanded by the will. He is not an "infinite object." He is immanent beneath nature and within man. Comfort needs "root-room." He appears unexpectedly in the created world.

159

> let joy size

At God knows when to God knows what; whose smile
's not wrung, see you; unforeseen times rather—as skies
Betweenpie mountains—lights a lovely mile.

The theological atmosphere of the nature poems appears
again, set against the comfortless state of the poet who,
like Coleridge, had been able to see, not feel, how beautiful the natural world is. Hopkins was much chastened at
this point, but he could recognize God once more in the
beauty of the world. God's smile is not wrung by a dogged
attention to moral choice, but suffuses nature as the dappled sky between mountains "lights a lovely mile." Hopkins was searching for that reconciliation of the demands
of duty and inclination that has been a traditional goal of
Christianity. Although he might never reach it—few
men do—he was hoping for something similar to Paul
Tillich's Christian reconciliation.

> When a child has a moment that we would call a
> moment of grace, he suddenly does the good freely, with-
> out command, and more than he had been commanded;
> happiness glows in his face. He is balanced within himself,
> without enmity, and is full of love. Bondage and fear have
> disappeared; obedience has ceased to be obedience and
> has become free inclination; ego and super-ego are united.
> This is the liberty of the children of God, liberty from the
> law, and because from the law, also from the condemna-
> tion to despair.[26]

Despite his recognition of the futility of the conflict
between his nature and his *arbitrium*, even a superficially
hopeful poem like "That Nature is a Heraclitean Fire and
of the comfort of the Resurrection" conveys a deep uneasiness. This long sonnet "with two codas," dated July
26, 1888, indicates its basis in conflict in the two parts of
its long title. Like the poem itself the title posits a proposition: "That Nature is a Heraclitean Fire" and adds to

26. *Shaking of the Foundations,* 136.

it a converse proposition: "the comfort of the Resurrection." The first part of the poem opens with the beauty
of an ever-changing nature, "million-fueled," and burning on with Heraclitus' single principle of fire produced
by strife; it closes, like "Spelt from Sibyl's Leaves," with
the vision of all, including man, "in an enormous dark /
Drowned," all, as in the univocity of Parmenides, blurred
by vastness, and beaten level by time. Juxtaposed to this
picture of nature—majestic in its never-ending process,
but horrifying in its indifference to man and indepen-
dence from God—is the "comfort of the Resurrection."
We again have the identification of man and God. The
human imagination does give birth to Christ in the world.

> In a flash, at a trumpet crash,
> I am all at once what Christ is, | since he was what I am,
> and
> This Jack, joke, poor potsherd, | patch, matchwood,
> immortal diamond,
> Is immortal diamond.

Yet the phrases "in a flash, at a trumpet crash" or "I am
all at once" show that the Incarnation here does not ride
time like a river. The second part of the poem is more an
assertion of belief in traditional Christian eschatology
than a recognition of Christ within nature and human
history. First, flesh must "fade, and mortal trash / Fall to
the residuary worm." The ultimate end is a timeless object, a diamond. It is not at all clear that Christ is born
in the *world*. Hopkins takes on His nature "at a trumpet
crash," apparently after death. The two halves of the
poem do not mesh; the comfort of the Resurrection does
not grow organically out of nature but is magically sub-
stituted for it.

In the symbol of the diamond lies a hope of ultimate
reconciliation. Although the poem does not, like "The
Wreck," work out the terms of human transformation in
history, the diamond, forming as it does out of organic
matter under intense heat and pressure secretly in the
depths of the earth, implies the possibility of God's un-

161

seen creation of immortality out of nature. The process becomes in a larger sense an analogue to Hopkins' life. Somehow, in a history beyond that of ordinary human time, the strife-born natural fire of Heraclitus may produce the transformed and radiant rebirth called for by the Gospel. Such a view does not resolve Hopkins' problems as the nature poems seem to have done, but it maintains hope in such a resolution, the hope of a man who was unable to resolve the conflict within himself but was unwilling to abandon the attempt. The similarity of Hopkins' later ambiguous attitude toward nature to Tennyson's conclusions in *In Memoriam* is striking. Hopkins' statement of the separation of God and man from nature, followed by an almost magical reunion, is paralleled in Section CXXIV:

> I found him not in world or sun,
>   Or eagle's wing, or insect's eye,
>   Nor thro' the questions men may try,
> The petty cobwebs we have spun.
>
> If e'er when faith had fallen asleep,
>   I heard a voice, "believe no more,"
>   And heard an ever-breaking shore
> That tumbled in the Godless deep,
>
> A voice within the breast would melt
>   The freezing reason's colder part,
>   And like a man in wrath the heart
> Stood up and answer'd, "I have felt."

It is perhaps fitting to close with one of Hopkins' best-known poems, a poem that is emblematic of his final state of mind. "Carrion Comfort," written some three years earlier than "Heraclitean Fire," expresses Hopkins' consciousness of his internal struggle by the metaphor of a wrestling match with God. It presents a traditional Christian maxim for those tempted to despair: God chastens those He loves in order to purify them. But the profound theological and spiritual schism from which the poem derives deepens this theme beyond its surface meaning and makes the poem symbolic of Hopkins' whole career. In accepting God's reasons for laying a "lionlimb" against him, the poet does not adopt a stance of passive resignation; he does not simply acknowledge God's strength in overcoming him. Instead, he actively "cheers," as in an athletic contest, and cheers, not just God's action, but the struggle between himself and God:

> my heart lo! lapped strength, stole joy, would laugh, chéer.
> Cheer whom though? The hero whose heaven-handling flung me, fóot tród
> Me? or me that fought him? O which one? is it each one? that night, that year
> Of now done darkness I wretch lay wrestling with (my God!) my God.

As Tennyson's confrontation with a larger-than-life Hallam in Section CIII of *In Memoriam* was also a confrontation with himself, so was Hopkins' striving with God in "Carrion Comfort" a recognition of himself. In the wondering questions, "O which one? is it each one?" we have Hopkins' vision of his divided self. Not only was the struggle between God and Hopkins; it was also between two separated personalities of Hopkins: Hopkins as Christ, immanent and creative in man and nature; Hopkins as Lucifer, animated by "will unwavering," but alienated from God by pride in himself and in his art. What made the tension even more unbearable was that sometimes Hopkins identified the creative personality as *Satanic* and the strong-willed personality as *Christlike*. It is small wonder that he should cry out, "O which one? is it each one?" In the continuing war between these apparently irreconcilable versions of the self lie the causes of Hopkins' personal agony. His "war within" is also a parable of nineteenth-century intellectual history in its theological struggle against deism and its literary struggle to re-establish the language of poetry in the modern world as both creative and cognitive.

IV.

LANGUAGE AS
CREATION AND COGNITION

These studies of two major Victorian poets reveal in their works a unifying theme—a motif of struggle that joins these two dissimilar artists on the deepest level while it seems to separate their art and beliefs on the surface. This struggle may be described not only in psychological and aesthetic terms but in philosophical and spiritual terms as well. More important, the many-layered conflict of Arnold and Hopkins was by no means limited to them; as was observed earlier, other nineteenth-century figures need similar study. We are just now beginning to apprehend the ferment below the levels of generalization that have so often characterized Victorian artists and their art. I do not mean that all previous critical estimates must necessarily be scrapped. I would hope that my studies support in broad outline the standard critical treatments of Arnold and Hopkins and complement them by viewing the same phenomena from a fresh perspective.

I have tried to interpret the careers of these two poets in the light of a crucial intellectual question: Can imaginative literature provide real knowledge despite the scientific revolution and the shift in assumptions about the roles of human perception and cognition that accompanied it after the seventeenth century? Related to this question is the problem of language itself. Is language an essential element in the process of valid cognition, or is it simply an abstract code, subservient to an autonomous reality that exists independent of it and independent of any human control? Not only were these questions of critical importance to the two sensitive Victorian intellectuals who are the subjects of this book, but they are still relevant for us in the twentieth century, whose current *patois* translates active *thought* into passive *input* and glosses *data* as objective reality and *imagination* as subjective illusion.

Neither Arnold nor Hopkins was able to arrive at an entirely satisfactory answer to this dilemma, although their work not only illuminated the problem itself but also, by analogy, suggested its relation to other problems we have come to regard as characteristically modern. Their work displays not only modern man's essential solitude and alienation but also his intense self-consciousness of this condition, "the dialogue of the mind with itself." In one poet we find a controlling myth of the impossibility of romantic love, suggesting man's helplessness in achieving meaningful communication and validly creative perception; in the other we encounter alienation from other men extended to isolation from God, as a deistic theology develops in logical parallel to the scientific revolution and the Lockian theory of meaning.

The irony of this gloomy picture is that the efforts of both men were in one sense successful. Although both Arnold and Hopkins were plagued by a continuing sense of failure and by continuing doubts about the value of poetry, their work remains a triumph of the imagination and a monument to the validity of poetic language as a means to real knowledge. If they sometimes felt their poems to be dead letters lost in the twilight of a darkling plain, we can see in them, to use a phrase of Wordsworth, "the breath and finer spirit of all knowledge." At times consciously and at times unconsciously Arnold and Hopkins demonstrated that poetry is more than an elegant amusement for the dwellers on Mount Olympus and more than a temptation to mere self-expression or triviality; it is instead the "fine delight that fathers thought" and thus becomes an important means toward a serious and fruitful "criticism of life."

INDEX

About the Author

Howard W. Fulweiler is Professor of English at the University of Missouri—Columbia. He received the B.A. (1954) and M.A. (1957) degrees from the University of South Dakota and the doctoral degree (1960) from the University of North Carolina.

His writings have appeared in *Victorian Poetry, The Victorian Newsletter, Mid-Continent American Studies Journal,* and the *Bulletin of the Association of Departments of English.*